MW01621004

I JUST WANT TO PAINT!

Mixing the Colors You Want

For Sharon,
May your color journey forever inspire you!

Please read…

Current printing technology cannot reproduce the same hues as painters' colors with 100 percent accuracy.

For example, the hue difference between the *green*-blue and *violet*-blue in my 6-primary color wheels (starting on page 18), are not as *green* or as *violet* as they would be in paint.

Even though similar color-printing variances occur throughout the book, following the instructions in each exercise will give you—on your palette and painting surfaces—the colors as stated.

There are also color variances in the reproductions of my paintings (starting on page 15), which appear darker than they are on canvas.

That said…please enjoy all the new possibilities of mixing color now at your fingertips.

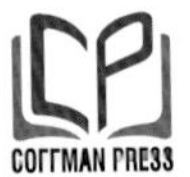

Colorfully yours,

Carol A. McIntyre

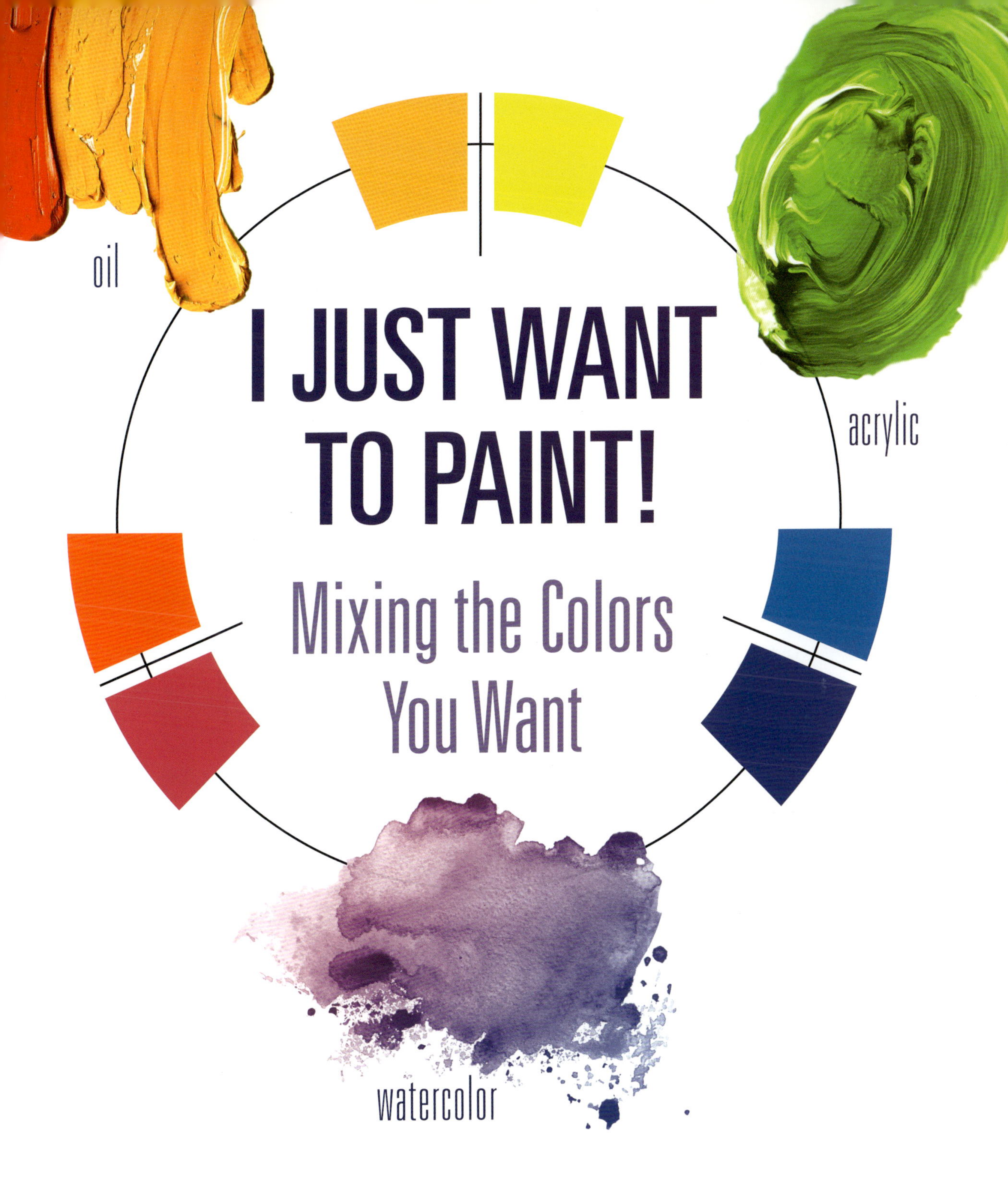

I JUST WANT TO PAINT!

Mixing the Colors You Want

CAROL A. McINTYRE

I Just Want to Paint: Mixing the Colors You Want!
By Carol A. McIntyre

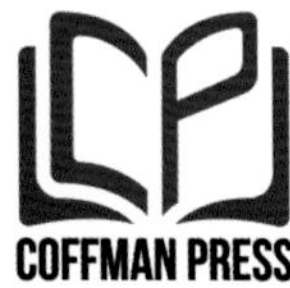

Visit our website at: CoffmanPress.com

Books may be purchased in quantity by contacting the publisher directly.
Coffman Press, PO Box 88073, Colorado Springs, CO 80908 or calling 719-510-0006.

Publisher's Cataloging-in-Publication data

Names: McIntyre, Carol A., author.
Title: I just want to paint: mixing the colors you want! / Carol A. McIntyre.
Description: First hardcover original edition. | Colorado Springs [Colorado] : Coffman Press, 2019. | Bibliography included. | Glossary included.
Identifiers: ISBN 978-1-7326280-0-7
Subjects: LCSH: Painting—Technique.
BISAC: ART / Techniques / Color.
Classification: LCC ND1470 2019 | DDC 752–dc22

Cover design: Gwyn Snider, gkscreative.com
Interior design: Julia Evans, http://tjstudiosdesign.wixsite.com/portfolio
Book consultant: Polly Letofsky, MyWordPublishing.com
Photographers: Carol A. McIntyre, CelebratingColor.com
Head shots by Ashlee Bratton, Ashography.com

10 9 8 7 6 5 4 3 2 1

Printed in China

For my compassionate and intuitive late mother-in-law, Emily Ann, who put the paint brush back into my hand when I was thirty-six, and her loving son, who has not allowed me to put it back down.

Contents

Preface

Seriously…*another book on color?* Don't we have enough available in stores and on the internet?

My color-instruction library holds over thirty books and DVDs, yet most painters seem to scratch their heads when it comes to *mixing* color. All that available material has not been enough to erase our mixing color frustration as we dive in, hoping intuition will lead the way.

About two years into my painting career, I wanted answers. Intuition alone was not giving me the confidence I needed as I dipped my brush into my paint colors. I was tired of playing a guessing game every time I went to buy paint and mix color. I was tired of mixing the dreaded color: *mud*.

As a beginning watercolorist, I began by asking a respected instructor to look at my paintings with regard to my color execution. He told me that I already understood color. *What?* I was dumbfounded because I knew this wasn't true.

Surprisingly, I discovered that most fellow painters weren't even interested in studying color. They believed the myth that says color mastery is intuitive and cannot be taught.

Alone, I set off…determined to seek out sound color instruction.

I lived in a large metropolitan area with a strong art community, yet nothing showed up in our local art centers or studios. I was flabbergasted and frustrated.

Eventually, I found a color course at a state university in the graphic arts department. I had to convince the professor to allow me, a nonregistered older student, to attend. This demanding, semester-long course was one of the most important decisions I have made in my twenty-five-year painting career because it taught me solid color mixing and color theory principles. It confirmed my doubts about the correctness of what that art instructor had told me. And it set me on the road to color confidence.

Before the internet, videos, and CDs, I devoured every book about color I could find. I created color charts specifically for mixing colors and was nicknamed the "color-chart queen" by fellow artists.

Then I discovered a small handbook by Moira Clinch, *The Watercolor Painter's Pocket Palette*. This 8″ x 6″ x ¼″ spiral book unlocked the final color mixing mystery I was seeking. Now I could confidently mix a bright or dull color depending on my original intention. No more mud!

Since *The Watercolor Painter's Pocket Palette* is predominately a picture book, I had to translate what I saw into practice. I had to move past the *what* of mixing to the *how*. In the process, I taught myself how to strategically choose two yellows, two blues, and two reds for a palette that opened up my color journey and gave me the mixing confidence I wanted.

After a few years of refining and gaining confidence with my system of mixing color—called the Balanced Palette System™—I started watching my fellow painters struggle with color. Soon thereafter, I offered live color workshops, followed by online courses and a written blog that generated feedback from painters who began to ask me to write a book about what I was teaching.

Motivated by my own painting and teaching experiences and the experiences my students have shared with me, I have become more and more passionate about helping painters end their frustration with mixing color.

You are holding the result in your hands.

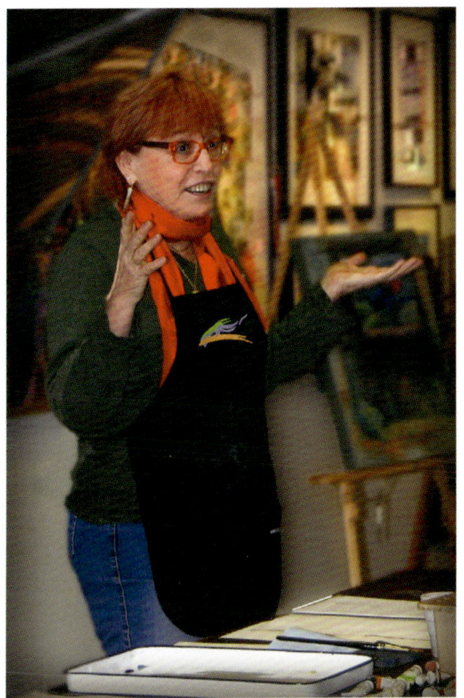

I have to tell you how helpful your class has been. With both watercolors and acrylics, I was struggling to understand why I mixed certain colors together that I thought would mix well and ended up with mud! It is great to finally understand which colors work well with each other!

—Maria Sanchez, online Craftsy student

INTRODUCTION

The Challenge: Learning How to Mix Color

Have you ever mixed a color hoping to get lucky with the result? Through hit and miss, you aimed for a color you wanted, but what you got is not what you saw in your mind's eye.

Argh! Frustration.

Or perhaps you tried a mixture of colors you heard that another painter used, yet that also didn't yield the result you wanted.

As a fine artist, I know how often this happens. I remember days of staring at my palette, looking at a still life and the color I wanted to mix and wondering, "OK, where do I dip my brush?" Often, I had no idea where to begin. And then there were times when my mixture turned out *yucky,* and I had to start over.

I yearned for a strategy for mixing. I wanted to feel confident in my approach to mixing colors.

We know color is the primary vehicle for expressing ourselves with paint. And we love color. Despite our efforts, it seems to be an elusive mystery, often impossible to understand.

Mixing color can be the bane of our painting experience. Why?

There are four reasons why learning how to mix color can be frustrating:

1. Painters believe the myth that color is innately learned and applied intuitively.

   Many painters buy into the idea that working with color is an intuitive skill. Hence, they resist studying color. This dovetails well with a sentiment I have often heard: “Color theory makes my head hurt.” Painters erroneously think that studying color is so analytical that it will block their artistic development.

   I disagree. I have seen, and experienced, how the study and practice of color mixing unleashes the creative spirit.

   Did any of us learn to drive a car or a bicycle intuitively? No. We didn’t. It required study and practice. Yet now we get behind the wheel without a thought to all of those knobs, dials, foot pedals, mirrors, lights, window washers, speed limits, stop signs, other drivers, and let’s not forget, utter fear. Driving eventually became second nature for most of us.

   Learning how to mix color is no different. Once you understand how tubes of paint—your tools of the trade!—interact with one another, you’ll have the foundation to explore freely and with confidence. After you have practiced the secrets to mixing color, then your intuition will come into play, and you will achieve the results you were hoping for.

2. We live in a world of too many choices.

   Walking into an art material store is like walking into a candy store. Every tube of paint sparkles. They cry out, “Buy me! Buy me!” Having choices gives us opportunities, but when we are learning a new skill, too many choices hamper our development by gumming up our decision-making process.

   I remember standing in an art material store and literally spinning while looking at all the paint tubes. I felt like I was stuck in a traffic roundabout, not knowing which road to use as an exit. So, of course, I ended up buying way more than I needed… because I couldn’t resist. And this abundance extended my confusion once I was in front of my canvas and had to mix *what*… with *what*? I became overwhelmed trying to decide which paints to use.

In 2004, psychologist Barry Schwartz argued in his book *The Paradox of Choice* that eliminating consumer choices can reduce anxiety for shoppers. I agree. The same anxiety impacts you as a painter, especially when you don't feel confident about mixing color.

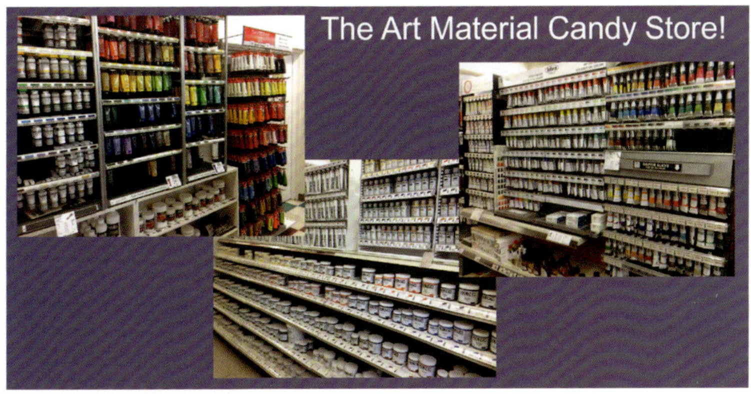

3. The language of color is not universally agreed upon.

Not only do we become overwhelmed by all the color choices available, but we also have to juggle the various words and concepts used to discuss color. For example, there are four different words artists use when describing how bright a color is: intensity, chroma, saturation, and brightness.

Another example is the misinformation swirling around tertiary colors. I've had art instructors define these as the "hues between a primary and secondary color" on the color wheel. In fact, a tertiary color is the *mixture of two secondary colors*. As a result of the common misinformation, painters fail to benefit from knowing how important tertiaries can be when wanting to mix rich, desaturated colors. The colors between primaries and secondaries are called intermediate colors.

As a color instructor, I help simplify, and clarify, the language of color so you have a solid foundation as you practice color mixing techniques in subsequent chapters.

4. Clear and accessible color mixing instruction—until now—has not been readily available.

Because traditional color theory is assumed to be one of the basic foundations for every painter, and because most painters—up to now—have struggled on their own to figure out how to mix color, most instructors are unaware not only of this missing information but also of their own biases toward color.

I have experienced workshops where color mixing is referred to in passing with only cursory attention. Or an instructor will lay out his or her paints for a painting demonstration but will not explain the strategy about why certain paint combinations work and others do not.

And more than once, I have attended a painting workshop and purchased every paint the instructor listed, only to discover that I didn't need to buy all those new tubes of paint. Besides the aggravation the purchase caused, it was also expensive—at a time when the workshop itself stretched my budget.

One time in a watercolor workshop, the teacher insisted we use cadmium yellow. During the class, I discovered that my tube of New Gamboge would have worked just as well. Ditto with Antwerp and Prussian blue; they are nearly Siamese twins, and I didn't need both.

As an instructor, why not list two to three yellows, two to three blues, etc. that can achieve the same effect? I had to laugh when one of my color students asked me, "What is so precious about cadmiums? My instructor insists that we use them."

I responded, "Cadmiums are not precious. You just have a teacher with a strong bias toward them. Several other paints look and mix similarly to cadmiums."

My goal is to map out for you the Balanced Palette System™—a color mixing system I developed with a set of easy-to-follow instructions—so you can ditch the frustration and really enjoy your relationship with color.

Because confidence is rooted in *competence* (not compliments!), the two basic keys to exciting results when mixing color are *knowledge* and *skill*. Master these and your color journey becomes a delicious exploration taking you down any road you want to travel.

That discovery led one of my students to say, "Carol, you have created a color experimenter in me. I would not have gotten there picking colors willy-nilly, as I was doing before taking your class."

Education is the cornerstone of liberty.

—Eleanor Roosevelt

How to Use This Book

You just want to paint. I get it. Once you understand the ideas and then practice the basic color mixing techniques of the Balanced Palette System™, you'll free yourself to do just that!

Keep in mind that this is a book about *mixing* color, not *applying* color. Once you learn how to mix color confidently, it becomes easier to understand how to apply it.

The principles in this book work for *all* tube-based media (oils, watercolors, acrylics, water-mixable oils, casein, gouache, etc.). Don't be fooled by the way color is taught based on a particular medium, because the concepts are universal.

As you read through this material, I encourage you to do the following:

- Work through the chapters in order because the information and exercises are strategically sequenced to build on one another.
- Keep the book near your painting area.
- Share your color discoveries with fellow artists.
- Refer to it as often as you want.
- Remember, dog-eared and paint-splattered pages are badges of success!

The following chapters and exercises for the Balanced Palette System™ will guide you closer to unlocking your intuition around color. I don't think there is a better way to learn than by doing, trying, and accomplishing what you imagined, *yes?*

Meet Paulette, Your Color Tip Guide and Cheerleader

Throughout the book, Paulette appears with color tips to encourage you to explore color mixing.

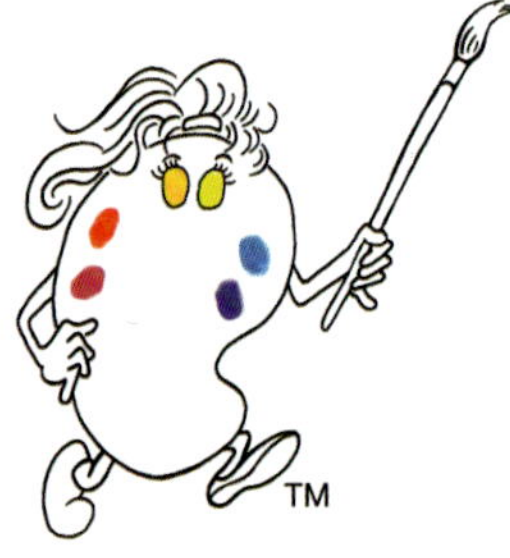

Paulette is an inspired tribute to my theatrical and fun-loving Aunt Pauline, who was an actress and prominent arts advocate in Southern California. She was also a significant cheerleader later in my life, living vivaciously until she was ninety-five years old. Aunt Pauline would have been tickled many shades of pink to have her name, Pauline, playfully merged with *palette*.

And like my aunt, Paulette knows that dressing appropriately for the occasion is half the fun, so she sports the *balanced* six primary colors every artist needs for color mixing confidence.

CHAPTER 1

Color Theory: Its Relevance to Mixing Color

I found I could say things with color and shapes that
I couldn't say any other way—things I had no words for.
—Georgia O'Keeffe

Early in school, you were introduced to the 6-hue color wheel similar to the one below. It's likely no one explained that this color wheel is the foundation to color theory, because at that time it wasn't necessary to talk about theory.

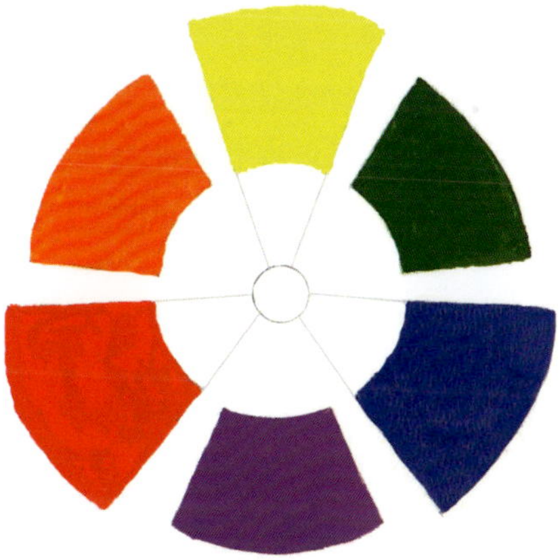

However, as adults learning to paint, understanding this traditional color wheel and its association with color theory is both indispensable and fundamental when we want to mix the colors we see in our mind's eye.

A Quick Color Theory Review

This color wheel evokes terms from the color dictionary, like *hue*, which is the first and easiest to understand.

Hue refers to the name of a color in a visually similar family of colors: yellow, green, blue, violet, red, and orange. Technically, it is the attribute of a color defined by its dominant wavelength of light. It is interchangeable with the word "color."

This 6-hue color wheel includes primary and secondary colors.

Primary colors: yellow, blue, and red, as seen here. They are called primaries because you cannot mix them from any other colors. They are the queen bees, if you will, and are the principal components that drive the color mixing engine.

Secondary colors: green, purple, and orange. They are achieved by mixing two primaries.

Yellow + Blue = Green
Red + Blue = Purple
Red + Yellow = Orange

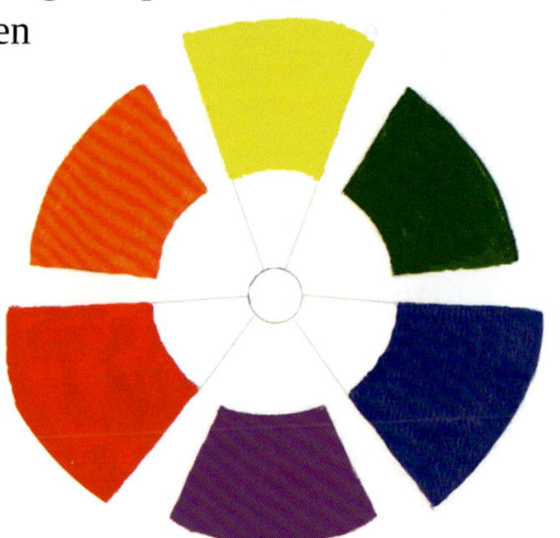

Notice that I always place yellow at the top of every color wheel; this is to establish a consistent orientation throughout the book. Think of it as the sun, which is always above us.

The Three Characteristics of Every Color

Every color—be it expressed through paint, fabric, metal, plastic, etc.—carries three characteristics. They are **hue**, **value,** and **chroma**.

1. **Hue:** This distinguishes one color family from another. It can also be called the parent or source color and is interchangeably used with the word "color."
2. **Value:** This is the lightness or darkness of a color. All colors can be described as being light, medium, or dark in tone, such as a pale blue sky or a dark blue sea.
3. **Chroma:** This refers to a color's purity or the brightness or dullness of a color. For example, the stronger or brighter a color is, the higher its chroma. The weaker or more mixed a color is, the lower its chroma. The chroma of a color can be altered by adding white, gray, its color complement, a dull color, or black.

Two other words interchangeable with chroma are **intensity** and **saturation**. For example, the yellow petals of a blooming sunflower are intense, whereas the yellow of a hay bale is dull or desaturated. Or you may hear painters say, "The sunflower is painted using a high chroma yellow." They could also say, "It's a highly saturated yellow." The reverse of this would be the terms **low-chroma** or **desaturated**. Artists also use **muted** when describing a desaturated hue.

The sheer range of words that describes this color concept can be confusing and somewhat frustrating, so I will use "saturated" and "desaturated" or "dull" and "bright" in this book as consistently as possible.

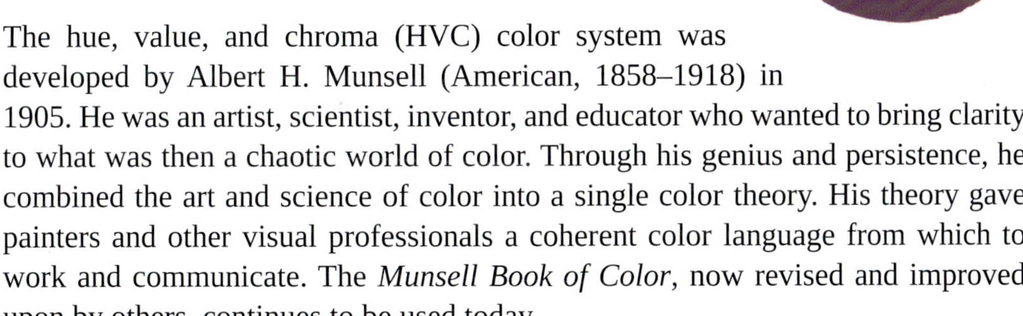

In the previous color wheels, all the colors are considered highly saturated.

The colors in this color wheel are dull or desaturated.

The hue, value, and chroma (HVC) color system was developed by Albert H. Munsell (American, 1858–1918) in 1905. He was an artist, scientist, inventor, and educator who wanted to bring clarity to what was then a chaotic world of color. Through his genius and persistence, he combined the art and science of color into a single color theory. His theory gave painters and other visual professionals a coherent color language from which to work and communicate. The *Munsell Book of Color*, now revised and improved upon by others, continues to be used today.

Complementary Colors

Another purpose of the color wheel is to show complementary colors, which are also known as color opposites, i.e., the colors across from each other on the color wheel.

I often refer to these as my "dancing partners," because they are the most important color partners when learning to mix the colors you want.

Too often artists spend only a brief moment learning about the magic of complementary colors, aka color opposites. Perhaps it's because we learned about them in elementary school, and so we imagine that's all we need to know. I strongly believe painters are missing out when they don't take the time to study and discover the untapped potential of color complements.

Throughout this book, I will encourage you to explore color complements more than you have in the past—to dig deep—after which you will directly experience their impact when mixing color.

Let's quickly identify these pairs of dancing partners:

RED	and	**GREEN**
BLUE	and	**ORANGE**
YELLOW	and	**PURPLE**

As mentioned, they are called color opposites because they are directly opposite from one another on the color wheel, as shown below.

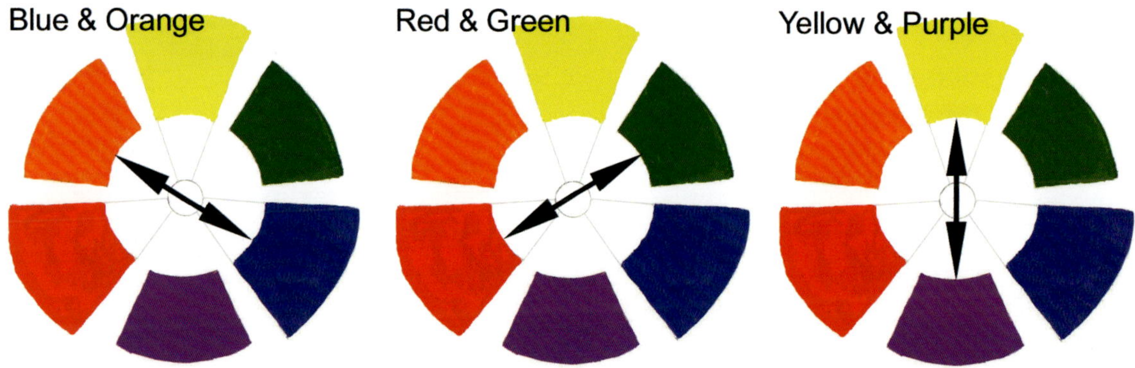

Because of their impact on your ability to mix color, memorizing these three pairs will increase your confidence and success in mixing clean colors. If you have difficulty memorizing them, another way to remember them is this:

The opposite of each primary color is the mixture of the two remaining primaries. These next three images explain what I mean:

1. Yellow (C) mixed with red (B) produces ORANGE (D), which is the opposite of the remaining primary, BLUE (A). Orange (D) and blue (A) are color opposites.

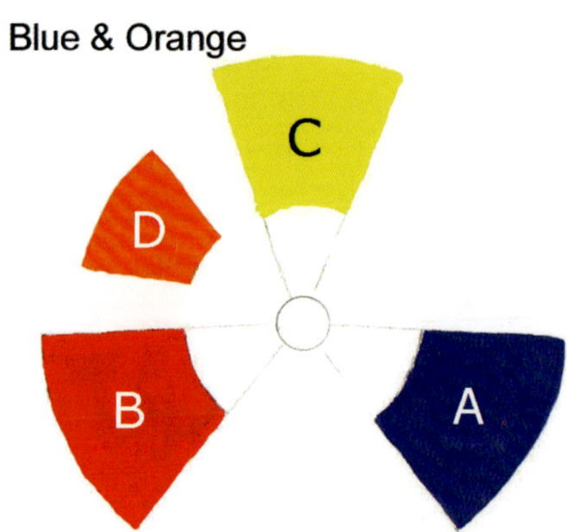

2. Blue (C) mixed with yellow (B) creates GREEN (D), which is the opposite of the remaining primary, RED (A). Green (D) and red (A) are color opposites.

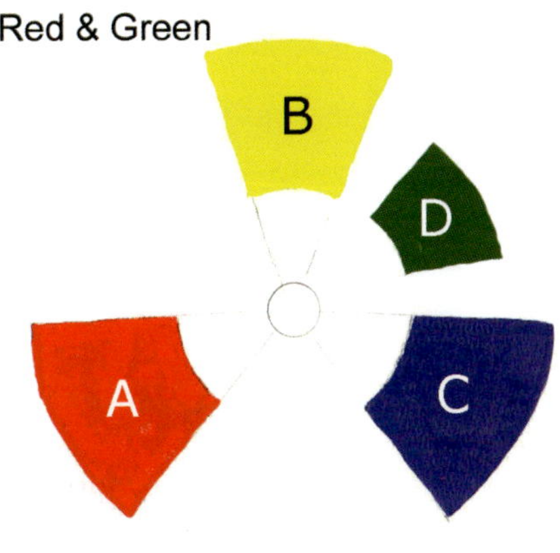

3. Red (B) mixed with blue (C) yields a PURPLE (D), which is the opposite of the remaining primary, YELLOW (A). Purple (D) and yellow (A) are the third pair of color opposites.

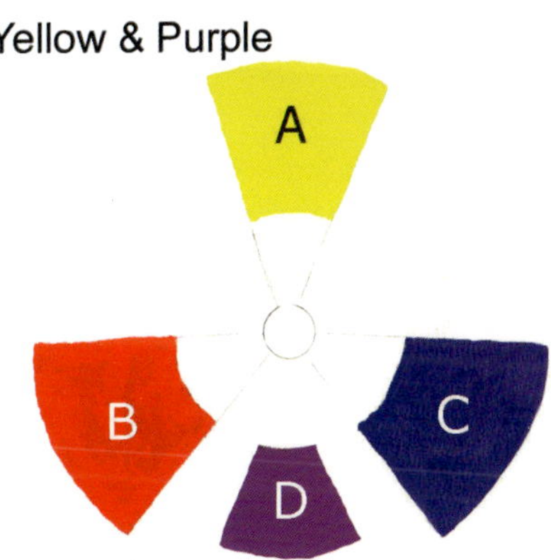

The three previous graphic images will help you see how mixing a pair of color opposites—or complementary colors—is a mixture of all three primaries. Only the *ratios* of the primaries used in the mixture are different.

Another way of memorizing these dancing partners is by thinking of the winter holiday colors of green and red, or sports teams such as the Chicago Bears—whose team colors are orange and blue—or spring flowers of yellow and purple, or the team colors of the Denver Broncos.

I wish there were a fun jingle or poem to help, but no one has created that…yet. Let me know if one surfaces. When I was learning about mixing color, I remember being surprised by how long it took me to memorize this: "Yellow is the complement of purple, red is the complement of green, and blue is the complement of orange."

These dancing partners show up so often when mixing colors that you want this to become second nature. Whatever memory trick works for you, take a moment to come up with yours or keep a small color wheel visible when painting. Through experience, I've learned it's worth the time and effort to do so.

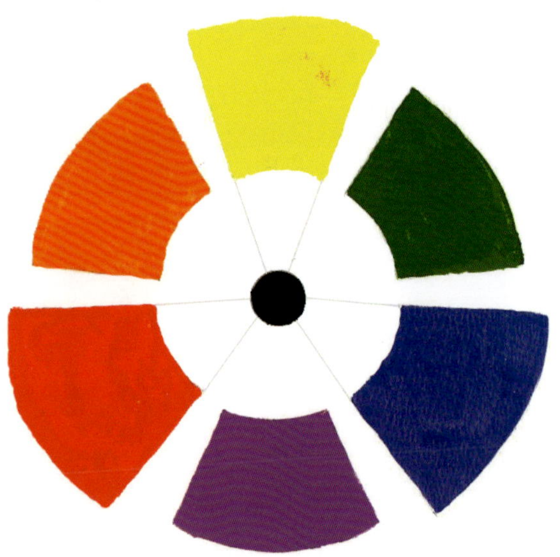

One More Color Wheel Item: Black

Mixing the three primaries together results in a black. In other words, when yellow, red, and blue mix together, they obliterate one another's original (parent) hue. I painted a swatch of a mixed black inside of this color wheel as a reminder of what results when all three primaries are mixed.

When you start experimenting with mixing three primaries, you will observe how these blacks are much richer than any black from a tube. Later, in chapter 4, you will discover how to mix yummy darks from various pairs of complementary colors.

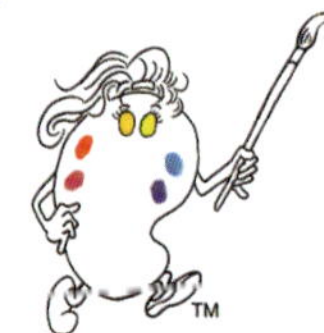

COLOR TIP: Mix your own darks and blacks for richer and more harmonic colors because tube black contains a dulling agent, which takes the life out of a color mixture.

Are you ready to apply this information in creating a working palette that helps you mix the colors you want?

Exercise Supplies

As the book progresses, you will be completing nine color chart exercises. Each exercise has been specifically designed so you can easily integrate the color mixing information you will learn as you increase your color mixing skills and confidence.

Suggested Materials

This list should accommodate what you will need to execute all the exercises:

- In a single painting medium of your choice, collect all your yellow, red, and blue tubes of paint.
- Ruler, preferably a 2″-wide plastic one
- Pencil
- Black permanent pen
- Six to eight sheets of 12″ x 16″ canvas or watercolor paper. Watercolorists can use quarter sheets, but it is important that quality, cold-pressed paper is used and not inexpensive, student-grade paper.
- Additional pieces of scrap paper may be handy for testing color mixtures
- Two to three pieces of 8″ x 10″ canvas or watercolor paper
- Flat brushes: ½″ and 1″
- Palette knife; this is optional for mixing with oils and acrylics
- Compass, or a 6″ to 8″ plate for drawing a circle
- Tubes of paint as described in each exercise
- Black ink or black acrylic paint (Note: This is only necessary when completing Exercise #2: Transparency & Opacity Chart.)

Chart Organization

As you complete your color charts, consider setting up a way to organize these color mixing gems so they are handy for future reference.

Some painters create a large notebook or portfolio in which to keep their charts. Others use a shallow plastic box.

My charts have never been uniform in size, so I dedicate a drawer in my studio for mine. Do whatever works best for you and your style of organization.

Also, date each chart as you complete it.

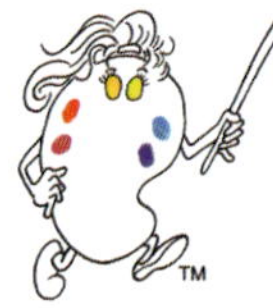

ONE MORE COLOR CHART TIP: If you want to keep a chart visible, use a skirt or pants hanger to hang it up near your painting area. And for oil painters, this is a great way to preserve a color chart while the paint is drying.

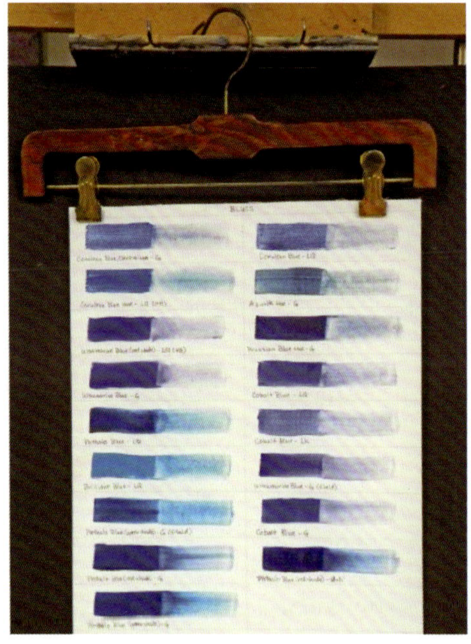

CHAPTER 2

Prevent Mixing Mud #1: Use a Balanced Palette

Discover the six tubes of paint you need to mix clean colors.

Mixing mud or *not* mixing mud is a choice. You may question this statement because those unwanted muddy colors have appeared in your paintings many times and you didn't intentionally *choose* them to be there!

When people see my paintings, they often tell me, "I love your colors!" Why do they say this? Because, besides providing color harmony, my paintings also have colors that are clean, not muddy. Here are two examples of "clean" color paintings. The painting on the right has desaturated colors, yet they are still clean.

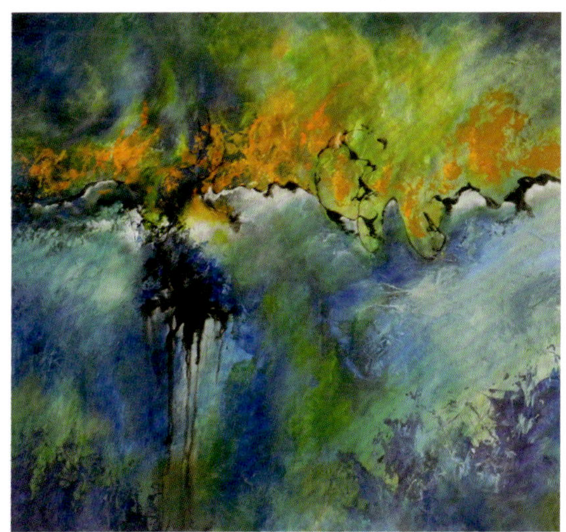

Riding the Waves, mixed media, 22″ x 24″

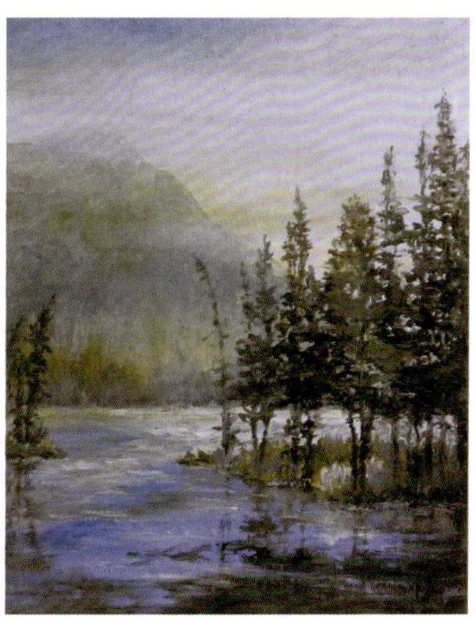

Through the Passage, oil, 10″ x 8″

The problem with muddy colors is that they have no life to them. And this sense of lifelessness doesn't relate well with other colors in the painting. Some describe a muddy color as similar to dirty dishwater or yucky paintbrush cleaning water.

So, what is a clean color?

It is an identifiable hue. When you look at it, you know its family of colors. It may be bright or dull, light or dark, yet you can name the color, such as red, green, blue, or yellow, as well as gray-blue, gray-green, mustardy, etc.

One of the keys to mixing clean colors is learning how to use a palette that is balanced. In other words, it means having strategically chosen primary colors that are available for you to mix virtually any hue you want. This balanced palette requires only a few colors to achieve this.

What's a Balanced Palette?

A balanced palette gives you a foundation from which you can spring forth and have a great time mixing color with competence and certainty without wasting time with the old "trial and error" mixing approach. Early in my painting career, I spent way too much time guessing which tubes of paint would mix what I wanted. And when my choices failed, I didn't appreciate feeling dumb or inadequate when I had to guess again for another try.

A balanced palette used within the Balanced Palette System™ I created, decreases color mixing guesswork. Learning how to implement this system begins in chapter 5. First, let's explore its core, which is the palette.

It's a working palette based on purposefully selecting two yellows, two reds, and two blues.

These selected six primary colors—much like the four balanced wheels on your car—will ride together in ways that will allow you to soar with color confidence.

This palette contains two tubes of the three primaries. These are not just *any* yellows, blues, and reds. Each tube is deliberately chosen by you to meet your needs and desires as a painter and to make it possible to mix the colors you want. You will learn how to choose *your* balanced palette as you proceed through this book. In other words, every painter creates a balanced palette unique to that painter.

If you are working with an opaque medium, then add white as your seventh tube of paint.

On the left is an example of my balanced palette with my oil paints laid out. In this situation, I am using a porcelain butcher tray. By the way, I lay out my acrylics this way as well. These colors, as I mentioned, have been purposefully chosen for my go-to, or default, working palette. On the right is my watercolor balanced palette. You will learn about laying out your balanced palette in chapter 8.

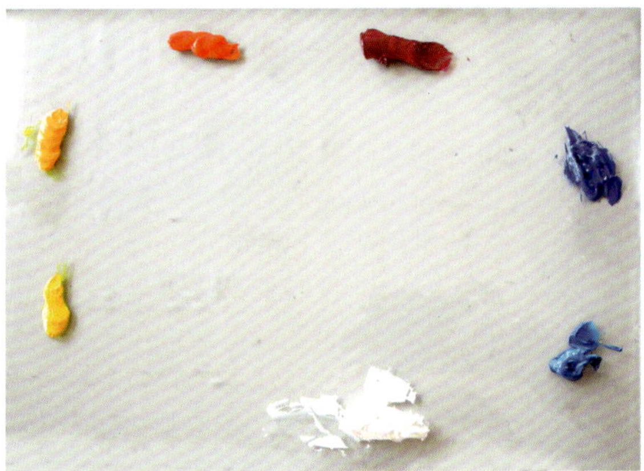

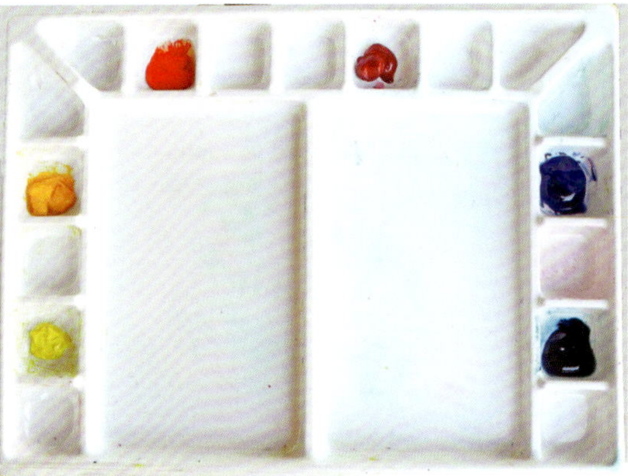

I will not list precisely which tubes of yellow, blue, and red paint should be in your balanced palette. Instead, I will provide you with guidelines and suggestions in developing your own set of paints. From there, you can decide on your color palette—the six primaries—that you want to use. I believe choosing color is a highly personal decision for every artist. Hence, I do not give out recipes or proclaim that you should use specific tubes of paint.

I strongly believe in your ability to make your own color decisions. When you own the process of choosing your tubes, you will be far more satisfied with your creations than if you are trying to replicate another artist's personal choices.

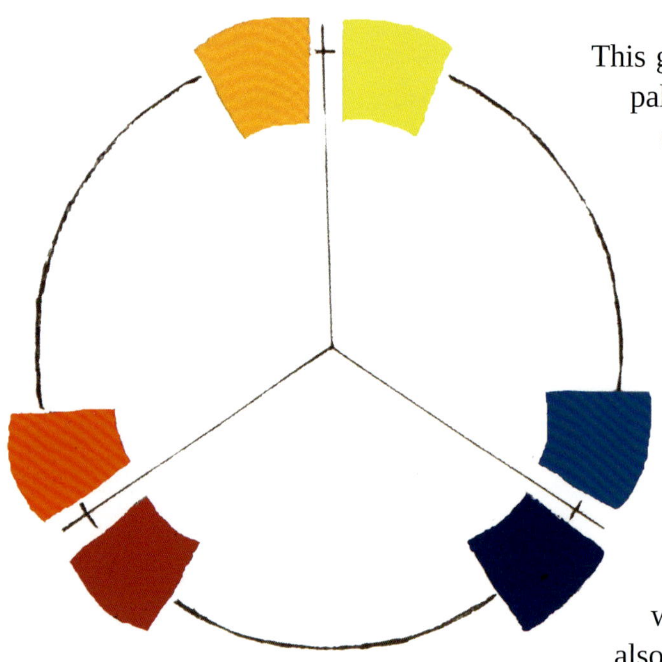

This graphic shows you a typical balanced palette, extrapolated from the traditional color wheel reviewed in chapter 1 that showed you *one hue* of each primary color. Here it has evolved to include *two hues* of each primary, with no secondary colors.

Throughout the book, I'll point out the abundance of benefits you gain from using this balanced palette.

By the way, the balanced palette, which is terminology that I coined, is also known as the split-primary palette, the two-primary palette, and the double-primary palette. Other artists and instructors use this palette, but most of them do not explain *how* to apply it or *how* to mix clean colors from it because they have not developed a corresponding color mixing system.

Simplicity is where painters operate best. The myriad of paint choices interferes with our ability to translate what we see in our mind's eye onto the painting surface.

Let's learn to drive this color mixing car by starting at the beginning and then methodically working up to full speed. OK? You'll produce more accomplished-looking artwork by mastering a few *key* tubes of paint than you will by fiddling around with dozens of tubes. It starts by getting hands-on with your paints.

Getting Hands-On with Your Paint Tubes

The best way to becoming intimate with your paints is by painting one swatch of *each* of your yellows, blues, and reds. Besides, there's something deeply satisfying when you see all your primary colors at one time in an organized manner. In this first color chart exercise, we are not including secondary, earth-toned, or black tubes of paint.

Exercise #1: Primary Colors Chart

Step 1: Gathering your primary tubes of paint

Collect EVERY tube of yellow, blue and red paint you own in one medium, including duplicates, student and professional grades, and all brands. Whether you have twelve tubes or fifty or a hundred, it is essential that your color chart display each of your lovely colors in all its glory. Having a color swatch of these tubes of paint gives you a valuable reference as you learn how to mix the colors you want.

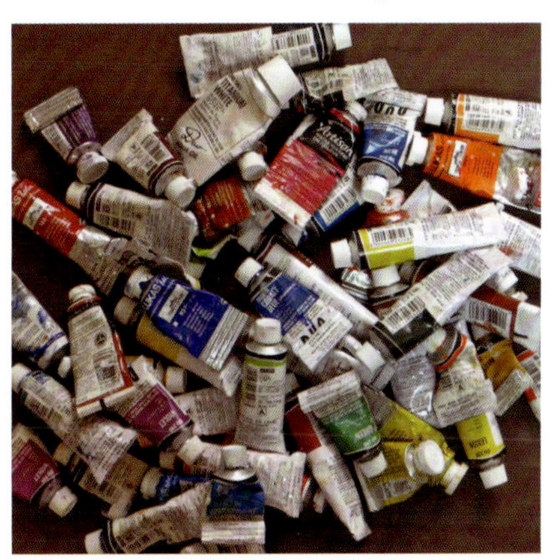

When you gather all your primary paints in a pile, it may look something like this. If you only have a dozen or so tubes of paint, this is OK. However, I know many artists tend to collect paint as they would seashells.

Getting to know your individual tubes of paint is critical to mixing color. This chart allows you to see all your colors in one place on a white surface while making it possible to see the nuances between the swatches of color. This is not possible to see on a painting palette or by looking at the colors printed on the tubes. It will also facilitate your ability to choose which six primaries to include in your balanced palette.

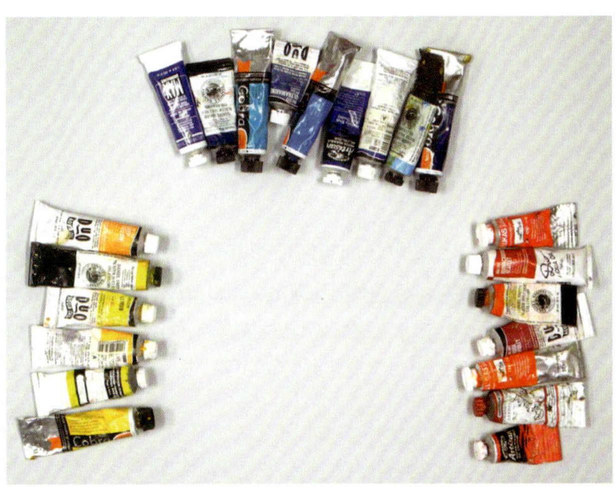

Step 2: Sorting your primaries

Group your yellows, reds, and blues into hue families, as seen here. If you are unsure about which pile to put a tube of paint into, take a guess. That the color is included in the chart is more important than where it is positioned.

> Oh, you may resist doing this chart. I know I did when I was first instructed to do it. I complained and proclaimed, "I just want to paint!" However, this is that important moment when getting to know your painting tools intimately will set you free. It is similar to knowing how to parallel park a car without dinging up your car.

Step 3: Listing your tubes of paints

On a regular 8.5″ x 11″ sheet of paper, write down every tube of paint color and its brand. This will help you know exactly how many paints you have for your chart. Don't leave any tube off of your list. For example, if you have two tubes of cadmium red made by two different manufacturers, write each one down. You may want to develop an abbreviation for each brand, such as GR=Grumbacher, G=Golden, LQ=Liquitex, HL=Holbein, WN=Winsor & Newton, etc.

Make a note of how many yellows, reds, and blues that you have.

Step 4: Drawing out your chart

You will need one to three sheets of approximately 12″ x 16″ canvas paper for this chart. If you are working with watercolors, you must use good-quality watercolor paper because student-grade or cheap paper will not accurately give you the information you need to learn about your paints. In this demonstration, I am painting each primary color family on a separate sheet of paper.

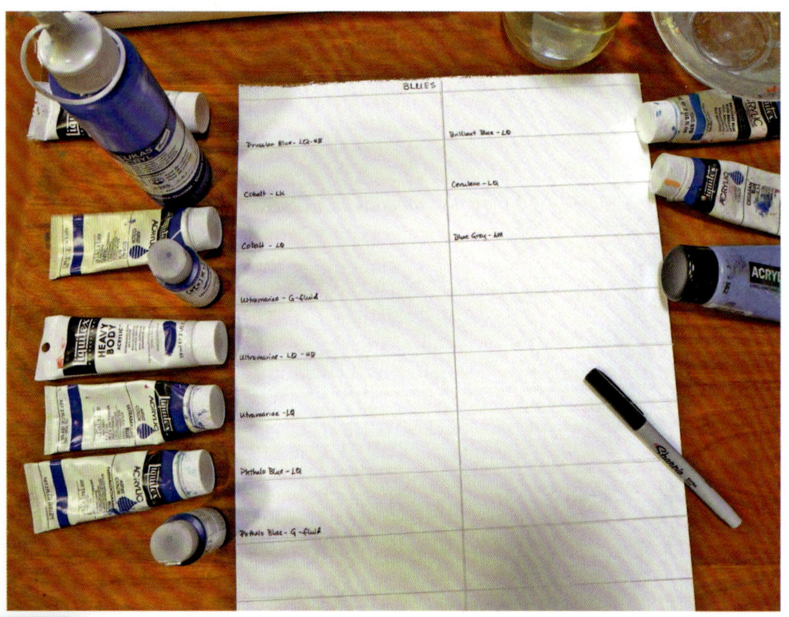

Turn your canvas paper vertically. Now use a pencil and straight edge to draw a line down the middle, creating two columns. (A clear 18″ ruler works well.) Next, draw horizontal lines every 2″ down the paper as shown here. This photo shows my blue acrylic paints lined up next to my labeled chart.

As you can see, I have written down the name and brand of each one in each box with a permanent pen. It is important to do this ahead of time because it is too difficult to remember which paint color went into each box. Trust me on this one! It is good to leave a few blank spaces as I have done.

Step 5: Painting swatches of your colors

Now you can start painting. In each box, using a 1″ flat brush, paint a swatch of every tube color. The boxes on your chart will be approximately ¾″ x 2″ in size, as seen in the example below. Apply the paint as you would in a painting. In this example, you can see all my red acrylic swatches while noticing that the paint thins out as it moves to the right side of the swatch. I added water to each. Watercolorists can do the same. Oil painters can add a medium to show a thinner layer of paint.

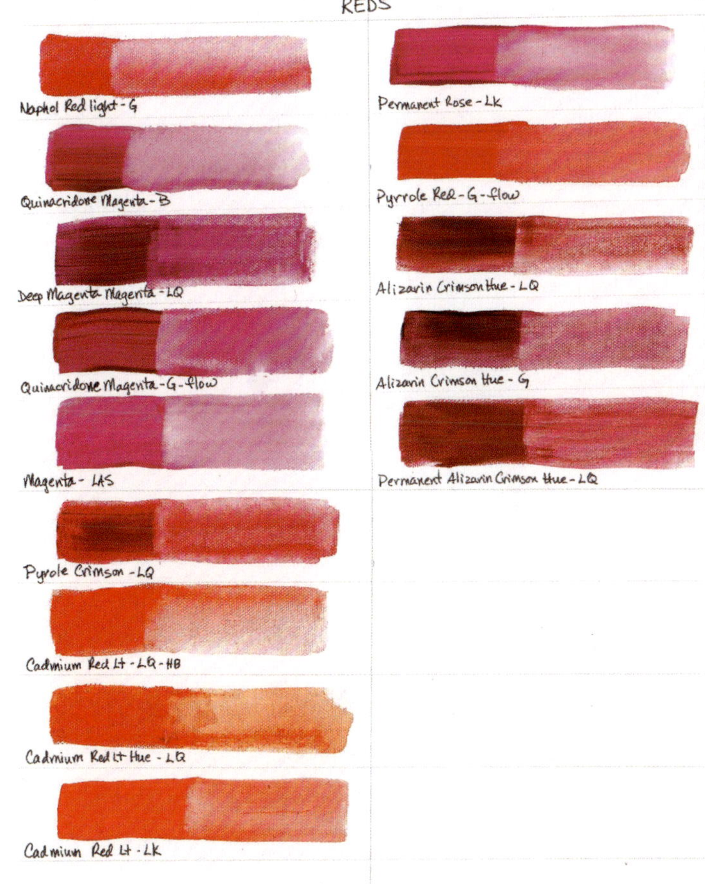

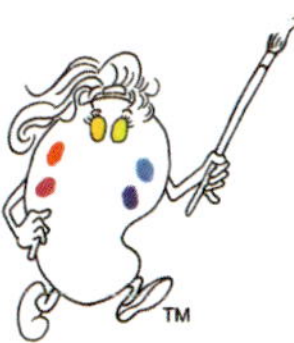

COLOR CHART TIP: Clean your brush or palette knife thoroughly between each swatch of paint you create to maintain the integrity of the color.

Each of the color charts in this chapter will be referenced throughout the book.

Step 6: Drying and reviewing your primary colors

Let the paint dry and study your lovely colors. Isn't it delightful to see all these sparkling jewels on a clean white surface? What surprises you when you look at your primary colors grouped together? Do you have tubes of paint that are very similar in hue? Is there anything else that stands out?

The Attributes of Paints

Paints in every medium have distinctive features. Like car models, they come in full ranges of sizes, shapes, quantities, and personalities. These differences can be the result of binders, chemicals, mediums, manufacturers' formulas, organic versus human-made materials, and the various liquids or mediums we artists add to a mixture. It's important to understand these characteristics because they can impact your color mixing as well as your artistic voice.

First, let's distinguish "paints" from "pigments." The various colors of paint that come out of our tubes are chemically produced with pigments. Most pigments are dry colorants, typically ground into a fine powder. This powder is added to a binder (or vehicle), a relatively colorless material that suspends the pigment and gives the paint its adhesion. Pigments are insoluble, and in most cases, the same pigments are used across all our painting media. It is the binder and sometimes an extender that differentiates watercolors from oils, acrylics from gouache, etc. In addition, paint manufacturers create unique formulas to represent their brands.

Pigments may be organic or inorganic. Organic pigments made from natural sources have been used for centuries, but today manufacturers are able to use synthetic organic pigments. As you may suspect, the quality of the pigments used is determined by each paint manufacturer.

The pigments, whether organic, inorganic, or synthetic organic, all have a code associated with them. These can be found on each tube of paint. For example, PB29 is ultramarine blue, PR108 is cadmium red light, and PY83 is diarylide yellow. If you are chemically inclined or just plain curious, go and look for these on your paints. You might find a couple of surprises. For example, Golden and Liquitex both use PY83 for their *orange*-yellow, but the former labels it diarylide yellow and the latter calls it yellow orange azo.

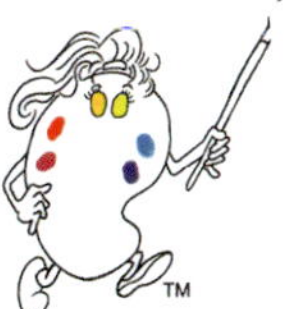

COLOR CHART TIP: Paint manufacturers like to lure us with sexy or fun color names. Look at the pigment codes to determine if you need the paint you think you want to buy. You may already have it in your paint box.

The Common Paint Properties

Previously, in chapter 1, we reviewed the three characteristics of every color. These are: hue, value, and chroma. In addition to these, each tube of paint carries its own set of paint *properties*. As per the information above, you can easily ascertain why paint properties vary. The properties are a) transparent, translucent, or opaque; b) tintorial strength; c) viscosity, or creeping strength; d) manufacturer characteristics; and e) modern versus earth colors; f) permanence, or lightfastness; and g) miscellaneous properties unique to a medium. These are discussed in detail below.

1. **Transparency Versus Opacity:** Paints are either transparent, translucent, or opaque. Each lies on a continuum from transparent to opaque. This property describes the clarity of a pigment after it has been painted and has dried on the painting surface. Some are quite opaque, and others have a see-through, almost glass-like appearance, whereas most lie somewhere in between. (See Exercise #2: Transparency & Opacity later in this chapter to learn how to assess this property.)

2. **Tintorial Strength:** This refers to the ability of a paint to tint or how strong it is when you go to mix a color. For example, many reds require a small amount of paint to create a vibrant color, whereas some cerulean blues are quite weak or low in tintorial strength, and you need a larger quantity of paint to achieve the color you want. This property is good to know when mixing colors because the quantity of paint you need will vary.

3. **Viscosity, or Creeping Strength:** This defines the ease with which the paint flows within water or a thin medium. Some paints spread quickly, whereas others are heavier and will barely move. This property is most helpful to know in wet-into-wet applications.

4. **Manufacturer Properties:** Every manufacturer uses a different formula to produce its paints. Most of us have favorite brands because of this uniqueness. For example, one brand will be thick or like toothpaste, whereas another will be buttery or more fluid. There is no right or wrong in choosing your favorite brands of paint. It's a personal preference.

5. **Modern Versus Earth Colors:** Originally all paints available to artists were created from earth, plant, or animal materials. These pigments were ground up into tiny particles and combined with a binder to make paint. In the twentieth century, additional pigments were produced using human-made materials. Most recently, many of our modern paints are made from coal tars and other petrochemicals.

   Our earth-toned paints tend to be more opaque. These include the siennas, titaniums, oxides, and umbers. The modern paints tend to be higher in saturation and transparent or translucent. They include thalos, quinacridones, hansas, and anthraquinones. Again, there is no right or wrong in using any or all. It is strictly a personal preference, yet it is important to be aware of the differences and to understand them.

6. **Permanence or Lightfastness:** This refers to how long a paint color will last on a painted surface over time under normal environmental conditions. Manufacturers are required to code the lightfastness or permanency of each of their paints. You can find this information on every tube. It is always recommended to use the paints with the highest lightfastness; otherwise the colors in your paintings will fade. I have seen this happen with beautiful paintings with which the artist did not use lightfast paints.

   Why are fugitive or nonpermanent paints produced? Illustrators will often use these colors. Their images are then used digitally or in printed form. Hence, there is no need for the physical illustration to exist over a long period of time.

7. **Miscellaneous Properties Unique to a Medium:**

   a. <u>Watercolors</u>:
      Staining versus non-staining paints. This refers to the ability of the paint to stain the surface of watercolor paper. Some paints have little staining capacity and can therefore be removed, whereas other paints cannot be removed at all.

Granulation: A few watercolor paints have particles of pigment that never dissolve in the water. These particles are heavy and sit in the valleys of the watercolor, providing a grainy or molted look. I like using them when painting a foggy scene.

b. Oils and Acrylics:
Sheen: This property describes how shiny or dull a color may look after it is applied and dries. Note that this is often altered by any medium that may be used with the paint. This shine can vary from brand to brand and color to color.

Drying time: Some paints dry faster than others because of their chemical makeup. The thickness of paint application will also have an impact on drying time.

All this paint information—the characteristics and properties—may seem like a lot to absorb at first reading. Once you get to know your paints and complete the additional color charts in this book, these attributes will easily become second nature.

It's valuable to know the extreme attributes of your tubes of paint. In other words, note the paints that have a strong tintorial strength versus those that seem to be very weak. Then notice if you have a preference toward certain attributes. For example, some painters adore opaque paints while others do not care for them at all. Enjoy exploring and discovering your preferences. Most likely, the majority of your paints will land somewhere in the middle of the continuum.

You may find it helpful to write in the paint property and attribution notations on your Primary Colors Chart, paying particular attention to the extreme ones you may have.

As promised, there is an efficient way to discover the transparency and opacity of your paints. Many students make their Primary Colors Chart at the same time as creating the following chart.

Exercise #2: Transparency and Opacity Chart

The transparency versus opacity of each paint tube is typically the most salient of all the paint properties. It is also the one most often discussed among painters.

Step 1: Painting black stripes

On a 12″ x 16″ canvas or watercolor paper, paint two to three lines about ½″ wide down the vertical length of the paper using black waterproof ink or black acrylic paint. Space the black lines at least 4″ apart and about 2″ from the edges of your paper. See the example below.

Let the black pigment dry completely.

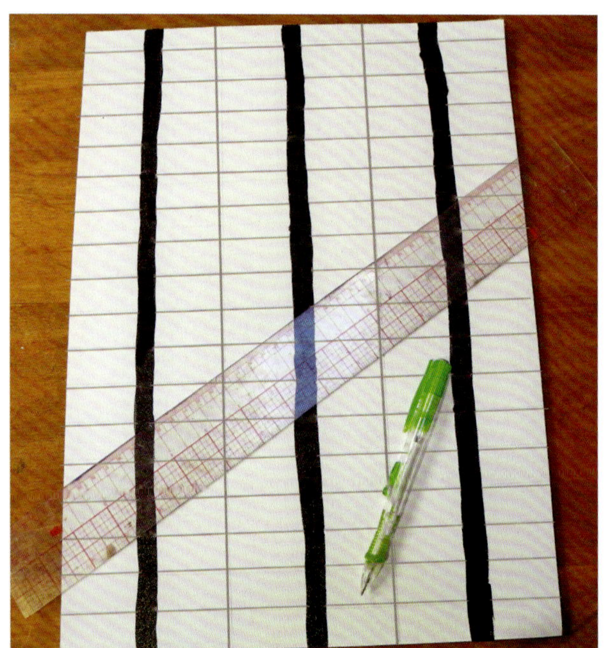

Step 2: Drawing out your chart

Next, draw horizontal pencil lines from top to bottom on the paper. You want these to be about 1″ deep.

Step 3: Labeling your chart

As with the Primary Colors Chart, it is helpful to label each box with your paint color and brand, and it is also beneficial if you paint the color swatches in the same sequence.

Step 4: Painting your swatches

With a ½″ or ¾″ flat brush, apply maximum-strength paint across the black lines in stripes of about 1 ½″ x ½″ in size. Apply the paint deliberately and straight out of the tube. DO NOT GO BACK INTO THE PAINT!

This chart shows which watercolor paints are transparent and which are opaque. Opaqueness is evident because the paint nearly obliterates the black ink or paint. The paint is considered transparent when very little of the black is covered up. By the way, most paints will land in the middle and are called translucent. The benefit of doing this chart is learning which of your paints is transparent and which are opaque; this can impact which to use for certain color mixtures and textures you desire.

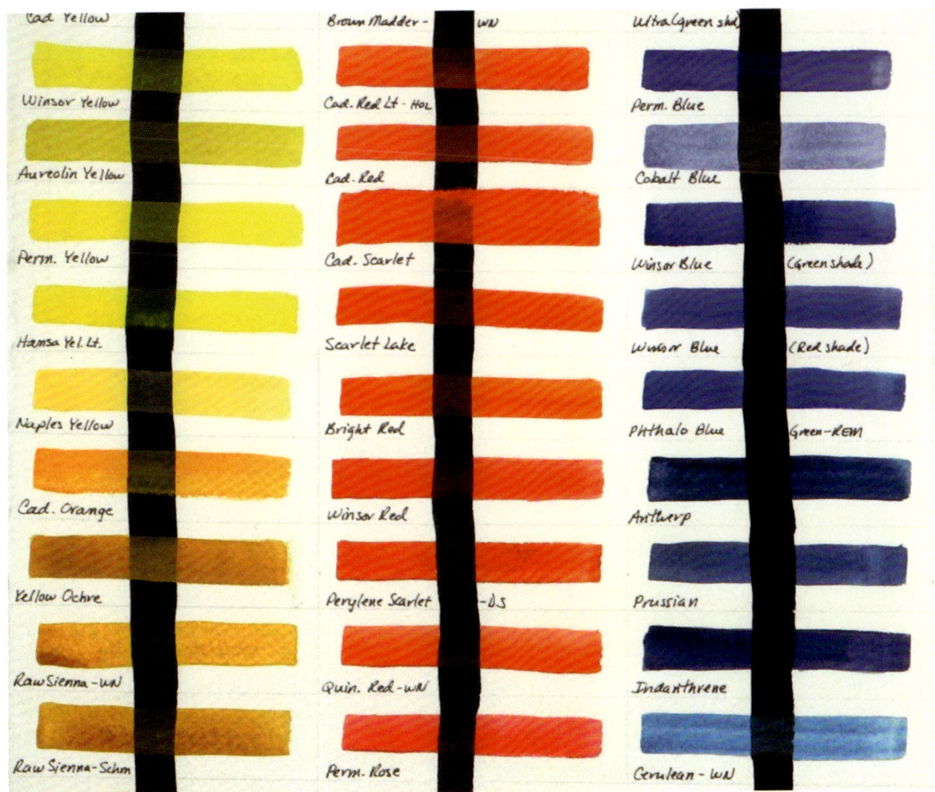

Here is an example of a Transparency and Opacity Chart with a small sample of acrylic and oil paints.

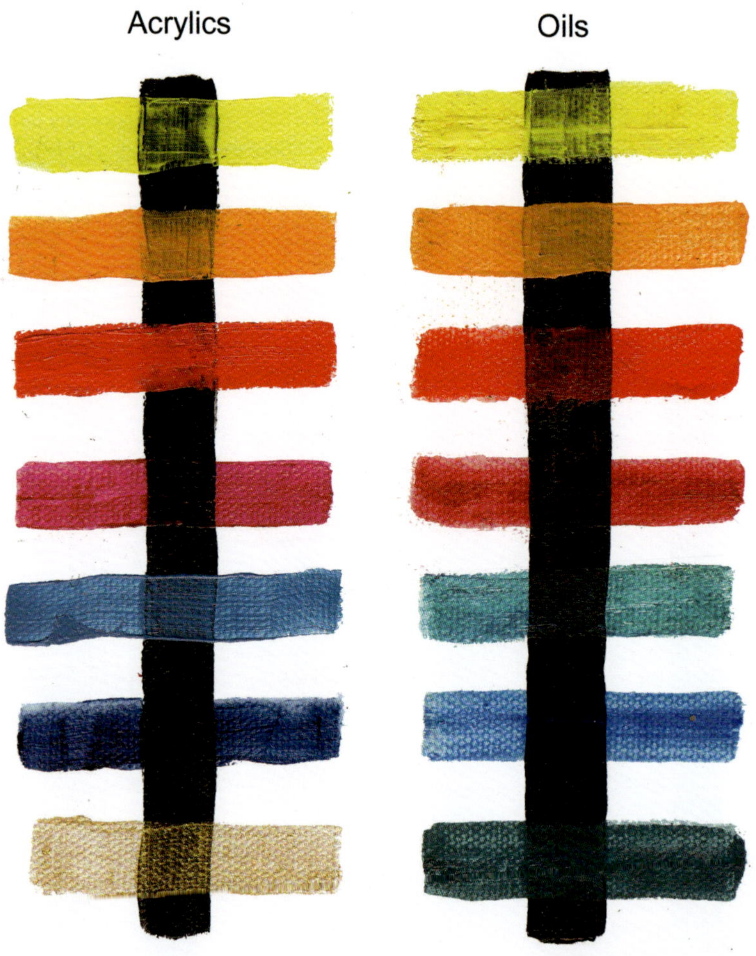

The key to doing this chart is knowing which of your paints are the most transparent and which are the most opaque. Perhaps you will discover that you do not own paints that fit either of these extremes, and that is fine. The more you paint and mix colors, the sooner you will realize that you have a preference toward one or the other or a combination. When you purchase additional paints, add them to each of these charts discussed in this chapter.

Are you inspired to discover more about your paints? Try mixing two colors—one a transparent color and the other an opaque color. Did you like the result? Now try mixing two opaque colors or some variation of transparent and opaque paints. Expand on this as you explore your paints.

Knowing your paints intimately allows you to do the following:

- Achieve the effects and textures you desire
- Identify the similarities and differences within a hue family
- More confidently identify the paints you want to purchase and those you can discard
- Develop your own balanced palette
- Discover your personal color preferences in hue as well as pigment properties/characteristics
- Increase your color confidence because you are becoming familiar with these vital painting tools

Questions to Ponder

- What is your reaction to seeing all your colors in one place?
- What surprises you when you look at them?
- What have you learned about yourself regarding your color preferences?
- Do you now see your paints differently? If so, how?
- What color seems to be missing or perhaps needs to be added?

In the next chapter, you will learn how to strategically choose your six primary colors for your balanced palette. This palette will become a part of your artistic signature and will help you effectively navigate within the color mixing arena.

Notes

CHAPTER 3

How to Identify the Color Bias of Primary Colors

For mixing, it's never "warm" or "cool." … It's "color bias"!

When learning about mixing color, how often have you heard art instructors use the phrase "warm and cool colors"? Most likely, you have heard it often. What does the phrase "warm and cool colors" really mean? And how does it pertain to *mixing* colors? If you have ever found this phrase confusing, I'm right with you. To this day—after twenty-five-plus years of painting—I still don't refer to a primary tube of paint as *warm* or *cool* when I *mix* paint.

It's not relevant, *and* it's befuddling.

Why we use color bias, not warm and cool, when mixing colors?

If not *warm and cool* colors, then what? I teach and use the phrase *color bias*. Why? Because it's a straightforward and simple way to describe a primary tube of paint as opposed to trying to describe its temperature.

What is color bias?

It's the hue that influences, or encroaches upon, a primary color. It is the adjective artists and non-artists use to further identify a color. For example, instead of designating a color as yellow, we often describe it as a *green*-yellow or an *orange*-yellow. A red is a color we often describe as a *violet*-red or an *orange*-red, and a blue might be referred to as a *green*-blue or a *violet*-blue.

The diagram below illustrates what I mean. Nearly every primary tube of paint available on the market carries another color within it. Or another way to look at it is that the primary color is encroached upon by a neighboring, secondary color. In other words, the primary color carries a *color bias.* It is important to note that very few *pure* primary colors exist.

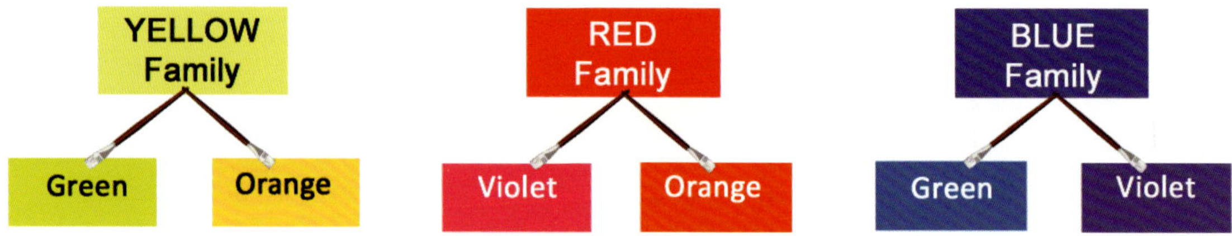

Nearly every primary color is biased or carries another color within it. There are very few pure primary colors.

Stating the color bias of a color is also easier to imagine in your mind's eye versus trying to imagine whether it is warm or cool. In your everyday life, for example, you might say, "He just bought an *orange*-yellow car or an *orange*-red sweater." You wouldn't say, "He bought a *warm*-yellow car or a *warm*-red sweater."

When mixing color, who cares if a yellow, blue, or red is warm or cool? Even though I might be committing heresy in the art instruction world, I believe this language complicates the process of learning how to mix color. When you are acquiring fundamental color mixing skills, "warm" and "cool" are words that do not provide a clear and practical place to begin.

> Vocabulary note: The adjectives used to describe color bias are the names of the secondary colors of orange, green, and violet. Hence, I use *violet*-blue instead of *red*-blue, *violet*-red instead of *blue*-red, and *orange*-yellow instead of *red*-yellow throughout this book. Using the secondary colors as the identifying adjectives is easier to understand when looking at the color wheel.

Knowing your warm and cool colors matters when it comes to *applying* colors on a painting, but this book is about *mixing,* not applying, color.

To mix clean colors, seeing and knowing the color bias (or leaning) of each of your primary colors is essential. Unlocking this knowledge will show you how and why you can end up with mud instead of the color you want.

These swatches of commonly used paints show off their color bias. When you look at these primary colors, you can see the secondary color that encroaches on their hue. For example, the cadmium red light is an *orange*-red, whereas the permanent rose is a *violet*-red, as is alizarin crimson.

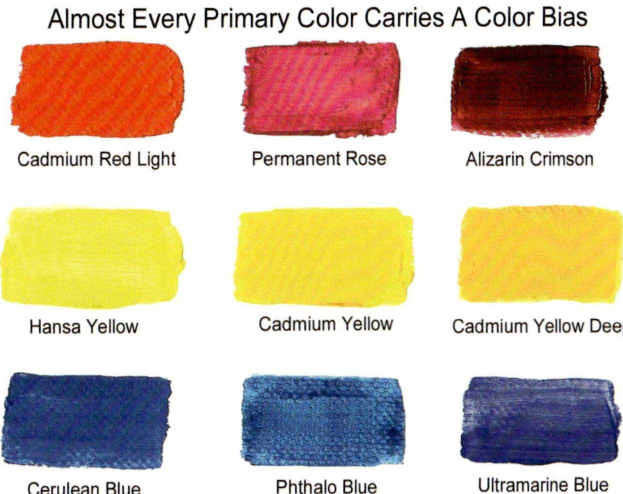

How do you determine the color bias of your primary colors?

You can identify the color bias of each primary tube of paint by reviewing your completed Primary Colors Chart. Previously I mentioned that it's easiest to see the hues of your colors when they are next to one another on a white surface, which is also how you can identify the color bias of your paints.

Exercise #3: Color Bias Chart

Step 1: Assessing each paint swatch

Let's start by looking at one hue family at a time and see if you can pick out the obvious, or most extreme, color bias within your yellows, blues, and reds.

Begin with the yellows on your Primary Colors Chart.

Pick out the ones that carry a *green* color bias and then those with an *orange* color bias. Select the yellows with the strongest color bias you can see.

Continue with your blues.

Pick out the ones that carry a *green* color bias, and those with a *violet* color bias. Select the blues with the strongest color bias you can see.

Finish with your reds.

Pick out the ones that carry a *violet* color bias and those with an *orange* color bias. Select the reds with the strongest color bias you can see.

Step 2: Identifying the color bias

Make a written notation on your Primary Colors Chart, identifying the paints that carry a strong color bias. There may be some paint swatches you are not able to identify with a color bias. That is OK. For now, set those paints aside.

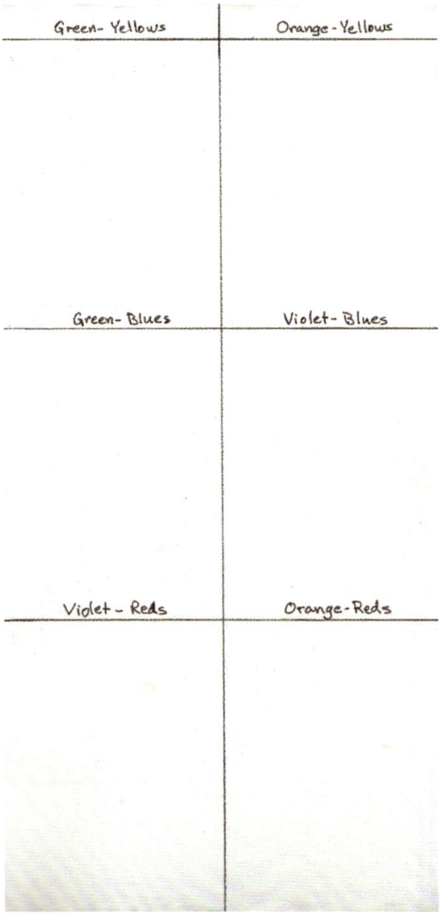

Green-Yellows	Orange-Yellows
Green-Blues	Violet-Blues
Violet-Reds	Orange-Reds

Step 3: Drawing your chart

With a ruler, on a vertically shaped canvas or watercolor paper of approximately 12″ high by 6″ wide, draw a line down the middle creating two columns. Then section it into thirds as displayed here.

Note: The number of paints you have with a strong color bias will determine the size of this chart.

Step 4: Labeling the sections

This chart gives you the six categories that represent the six primaries you will need to create a balanced palette later on.

In the left column, as per the example, label the top section as Green-Yellows, the middle section as Green-Blues, and the last section as Violet-Reds.

In the right column, label the top section as Orange-Yellows, the middle as Violet-Blues, and the last section as Orange-Reds.

Step 5: Painting your swatches

Following the labeled sections, paint the corresponding swatches of paint starting with your yellows. Paint one example of each *green*-yellow you have and then the *orange*-yellows.

Continue this process with your *green*-blues and *violet*-blues. End with painting swatches of your *violet*-reds and *orange*-reds. Below is an example of a Color Bias Chart.

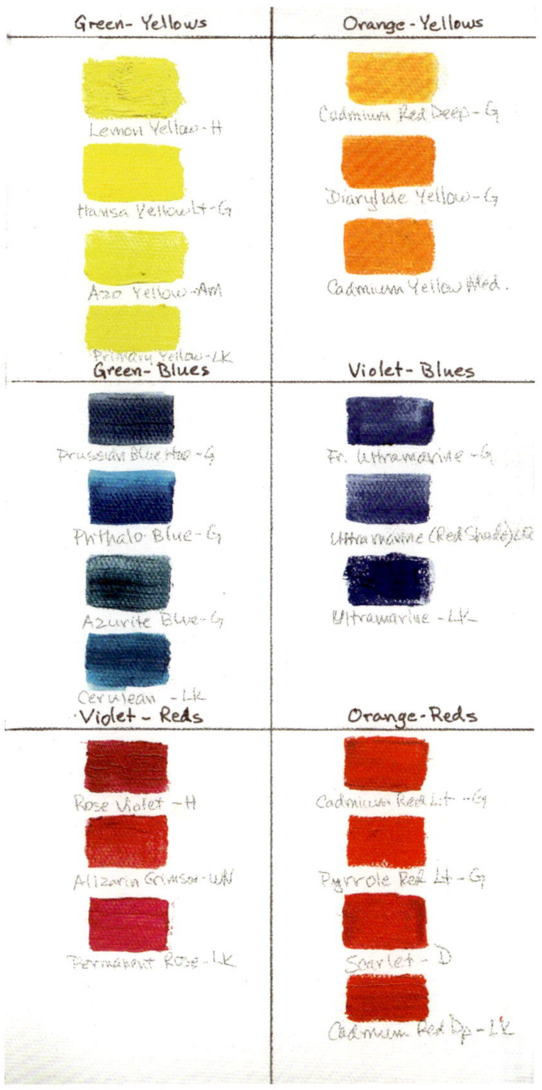

Step 6: Reviewing your chart

Do you have a primary color for each of these six sections? If you do not have a tube of paint for any one of these six categories, then this means you need to purchase one. Oh boy! Time to go to the candy store! For example, if you do not own a *violet*-red, please go get one. You will need it when it comes time to create your balanced palette.

When you were analyzing your Primary Colors Chart, you may have noticed paints that did not carry a strong color bias. One such popular color is cobalt. It does not lean strongly one way or another. For the time being, I am going to request you leave it alone.

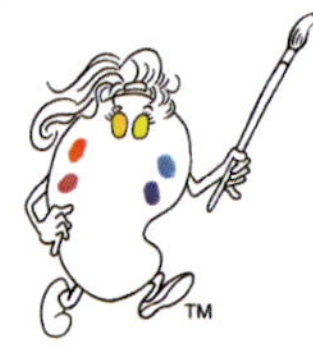

COLOR TIP: Almost all available blues carry a green bias. Very few carry a violet bias.

With this Color Bias Chart, you are ready to start putting together your balanced palette.

Painting a color wheel for your balanced palette is the best way to start.

Exercise #4: *Your* Balanced Palette Color Wheel

Step 1: Choosing your yellows, reds, and blues

Refer to your Color Bias Chart above and choose the following for your initial balanced palette:

a) two yellows—a *green*-yellow and an *orange*-yellow;
b) two blues—a *green*-blue and a *violet*-blue; and
c) two reds—a *violet*-red and an *orange*-red.

There are no right or wrong choices. This is *your* personal palette signifying one aspect of your artistic vision.

The important decision is to strategically choose six primary colors, with each one of the six carrying a strong color bias.

In the end, there is no rule that says you can only have one balanced palette. However, for the remainder of the book and its exercises, I encourage you to use a "beginning" balanced palette with its one set of six primaries. We'll discuss additional balanced palettes down the road.

Step 2: Drawing out a color wheel for your balanced palette

Once you have chosen your primary colors, create a color wheel similar to the one at right, using a 12″ x 16″ piece of canvas or watercolor paper.

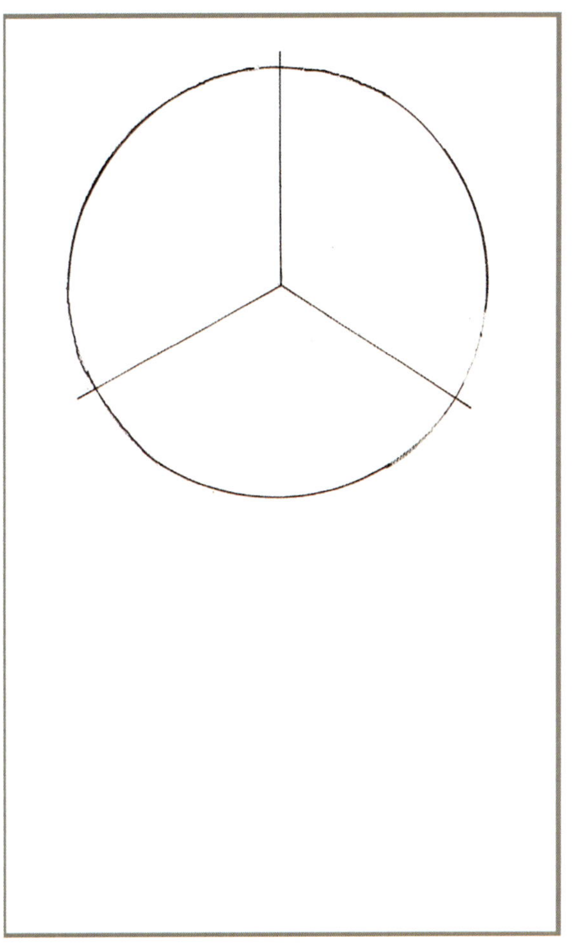

Draw the circle in the top half of the paper because you will need the bottom half when we discuss how to mix bright and dull secondary colors. A plate or compass is an easy way to make a 5–6″-wide circle.

After drawing in your circle, draw in straight lines marked off in thirds, as seen here.

Painting a color wheel may seem like an overly simple or mundane exercise, but this is a different kind of color wheel, with which you need to display the set of six primary colors you chose for your beginning balanced palette.

This balanced palette color wheel will be your main mixing reference tool for the remainder of this book.

Step 3: Labeling your color wheel

Next, label the location of the primaries—yellow, blue, and red. It is important that yellow is at the top of the color wheel, with red to the left and blue to the right.

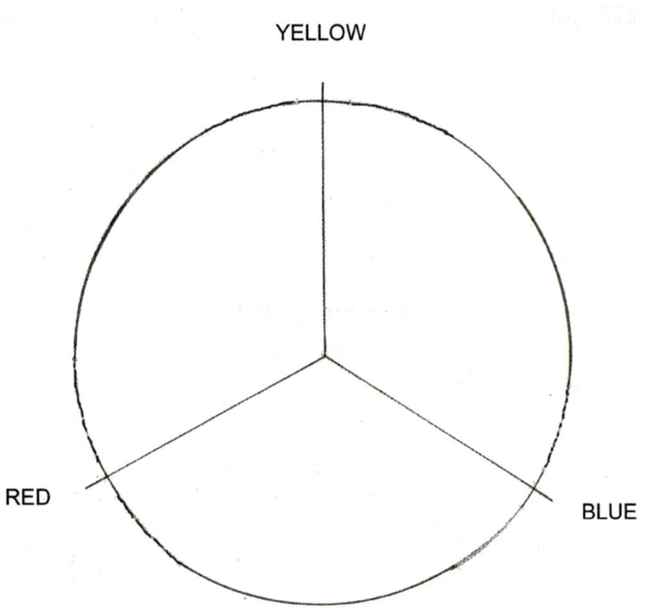

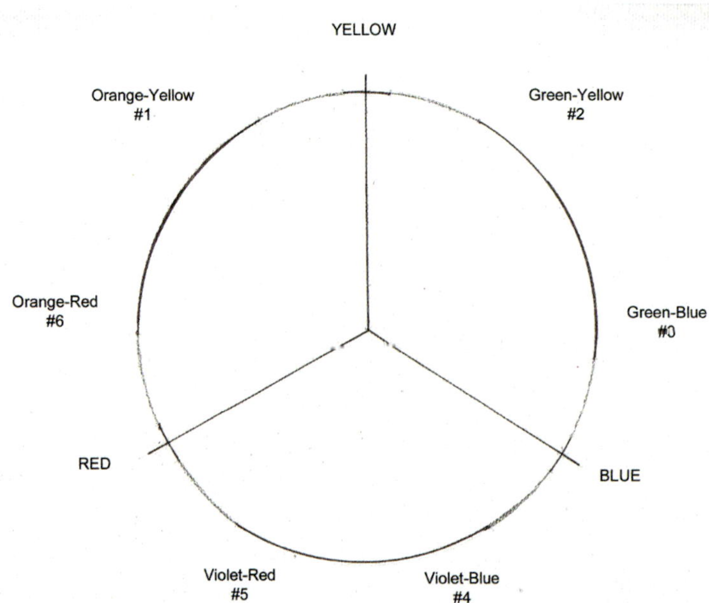

Step 4: Continue labeling your color wheel

The next step is to label the location of your set of six primary colors.

In the example to the left, they are labeled according to their respective color biases. They are also numbered from #1 to #6, starting with the *orange*-yellow and going around the color wheel clockwise.

This specific numbering system is very important because it will be used when we implement strategies for mixing various colors in future chapters.

Step 5: Painting your primary colors

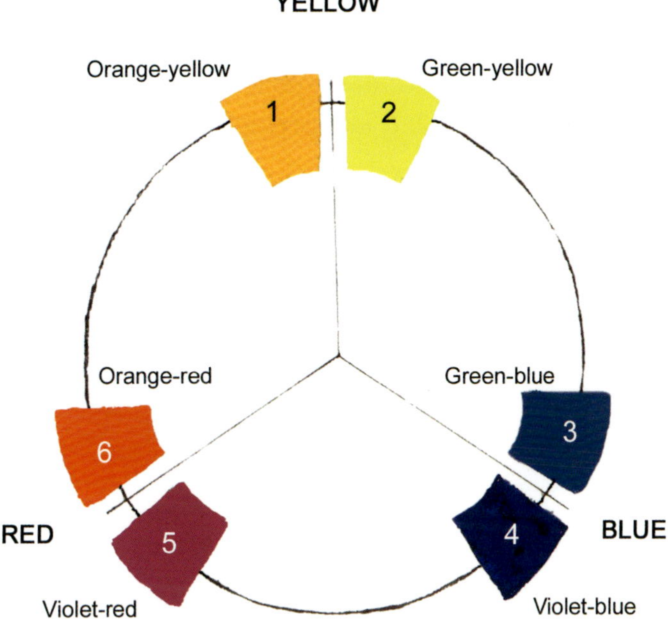

Grab your set of six primary colors and paint a swatch of each. Start with your *orange-yellow* (#1) and then work your way around the color wheel.

Be sure you keep your brush clean between painting swatches to maintain the integrity of each primary. There's no need to be neat and precise like I am with my color wheel; the important task is creating a color wheel of *your* balanced palette colors.

In my example, I have used photographic software to place the numbers within each swatch of paint to make those numbers easier to read for this book format.

Be sure to label your primary colors with their hue name and brand, either directly around this color wheel or listed along the side.

Step 6: Reviewing your color wheel

Congratulations. You have created a color wheel for your first balanced palette! This is the first step in understanding the Balanced Palette System of mixing color.

You are now ready to start using this color wheel, which is your foundation for learning how to mix the clean colors you want.

This first set of six primaries may change after you have started mixing with them and learned that you want different results. Doing the exercises in this book will give you the information you need to make decisions about which set of primaries you may want in a future balanced palette. For now, just start with your original six.

Here is a list of primaries that typically carry strong color biases in all media, though the color names may vary. This is a short list to provide examples to consider for future balanced palettes and is not a substitute for exploring your paints now and identifying your personalized set of six primary colors.

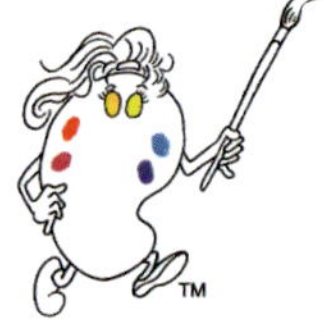

COLOR TIP: As much as I want you to explore and discover on your own, I also want to give you examples of primaries that carry a strong color bias. So, with the caveat that this does not replace your own selection, here is a short list:

YELLOWS **Orange-yellows:** Indian yellow, cadmium yellow deep, New Gamboge, diarylide
Green-yellows: lemon yellow, Hansa yellow light, cadmium yellow light, cadmium yellow pale, aureolin

BLUES **Green-blues:** Prussian, cerulean, phthalo blue, manganese
Violet-blues: French Ultramarine blue, permanent blue, phthalo blue red shade

REDS **Violet-reds:** rose, permanent rose, magenta, crimson red, alizarin crimson
Orange-reds: scarlet, vermilion, cadmium red light

We live in an art world with an abundance of tubes of paint that tantalize us like pieces of candy. They have interesting names and hues varying from manufacturer to manufacturer. Do not be swayed by this. Taking the time to paint swatches of each tube on your Primary Colors Chart will give you a way to identify the best balanced palette for you. Some manufacturers seduce us with cute and creative names when, in reality, they are just repackaged.

When I started working with my balanced palette, I was afraid that I was missing out on something because I had so many tubes of paint in my paint box. I wondered if I could create successful paintings with only six primaries and neglect those unused paints. To my surprise, I soon experienced a sense of freedom and confidence I had not expected from using my system.

I learned that expressing my artistic vision became easier and more efficient when I practiced the guidelines in this book. I also discovered that I didn't need to waste money on tubes of paint I didn't need!

If I wanted to add one of my "neglected" tubes of paint, I learned how to evaluate it and decide whether I wanted to use it for mixing…or not. These discoveries became life changing.

Each of you will find the six primary colors that work best for you and what you want to express in your paintings. This is why one color palette does not work for all. Go ahead and experiment, but be sure you understand your initial six colors before continuing to try out different combinations for additional balanced palettes.

Before I set you up to mix from your initial balanced palette, we have to discuss an essential color mixing concept—complementary colors.

Since complementary colors are ignored too often, get ready to be surprised by the powerful impact they have on mixing the colors you want.

Notes

CHAPTER 4

Complementary Colors: Let the Dance Begin

One secret for intentionally mixing mud when you need it

Complementary colors—also referred to as *color opposites*—are a well-known color concept that we introduced in chapter 1. In fact, most of us learned about them when we were quite young: **purple is the opposite of yellow**, **orange is the opposite of blue**, and **green is the opposite of red**.

Before we learn more about the role complementary colors play in color mixing, I want to clear up a frequent misspelling.

Back in my early days of painting, I struggled to remember the correct spelling of *complementary*. I was never clear about whether it was spelled with an "i" or an "e." It's easy to be confused because the English language spells this word both ways. Complimentary, with an "i," means "expressing praise" as well as "giving something away at no cost." For example, an art material store may offer a *complimentary* tube of paint after purchasing six brushes.

Complementary color is spelled with an "e" because the root word for compl**e**mentary is *complete*. As we talked about in chapter 1, the mixture of any pair of complementary colors uses a different ratio of the three primaries—yellow, blue, and red. In other words, the *complete* color wheel is being used. Hence, we refer to them as complementary colors.

This idea of "complete" is reinforced by a dictionary's definition of *complementary*: 1. combining in such a way as to enhance or emphasize the qualities of each other or another; 2. something that fills up, completes, or makes perfect.

Mixing Complementary Colors

Knowing and understanding complementary colors are fundamental to *all* your color mixing.

Why?

When any two complementary colors are mixed together, each one of the two begins to dull or neutralize the other. In other words, the colors start to desaturate in hue.

Complementary colors have a special relationship in mixing because of the following:

- One partner does not carry the color of the other.
- The hue in one complementary color "cancels," or neutralizes, the opposite color when mixed.

To elaborate on the first bullet, look at the complementary colors of blue and orange below. There is no orange hue in the blue, and there is no blue hue in the orange.

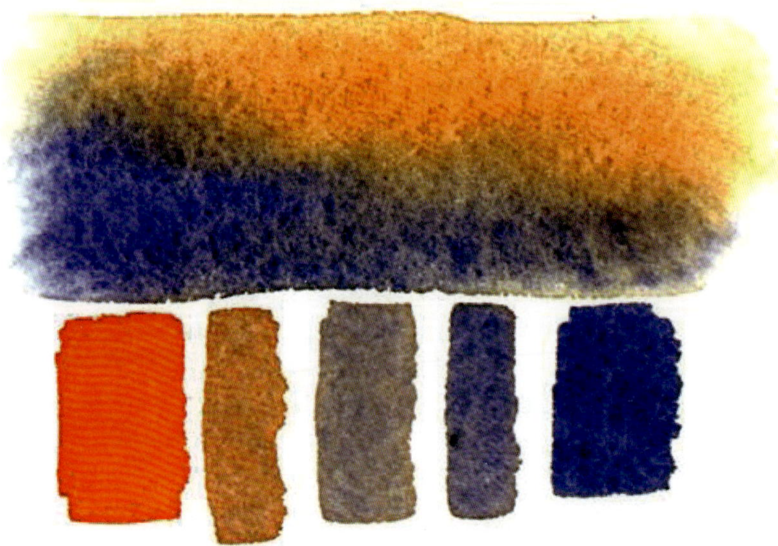

You could say that there is no other color on the color wheel that is as different from blue as orange. The same can be said when comparing green with red, and purple with yellow.

Let's see how well different mixtures of complementary colors dance together!

The previous example, in watercolor, mixes a complementary pairing of an orange and a blue. The top swatch demonstrates how a wet-into-wet application causes these complementary colors to float into each other. Can you see the desaturated colors where the orange and blue meet? Isn't it interesting to see how they almost dance where the colors merge?

The five color swatches below the wet-into-wet show you what happens when a pair of orange and blue is mixed with different ratios. The middle swatch is an equal combination of the two complementary colors. The swatches on either side of the middle show how quickly the original, bright color loses its saturation once it's mixed with its opposite.

Do you, or would you, consider these duller colors mud? They might be if you were not expecting the decrease in color saturation, but the duller version might be exactly the color you need in a particular painting.

When you are consciously aware of the possibilities, these duller mixtures are welcomed. Complementary colors create a vital range of colors that can be desaturated in varying degrees, from slight to significant, depending on your vision.

> Note: If you want to know which colors, or names of tube paints, are in my examples, remember, it doesn't matter which colors I selected for this book. What matters are the colors you select for your personalized palette—the foundation of your visual voice.
>
> Refer back to chapter 2 to become more intimate with your tubes of paint. In later chapters, we'll go into more depth about your color choices and how this impacts your work.
>
> Also, because I include different media in my examples, a hue in watercolor or oil may differ slightly from a color or tube of paint in acrylic. In other words, knowing what I have selected would not be useful.

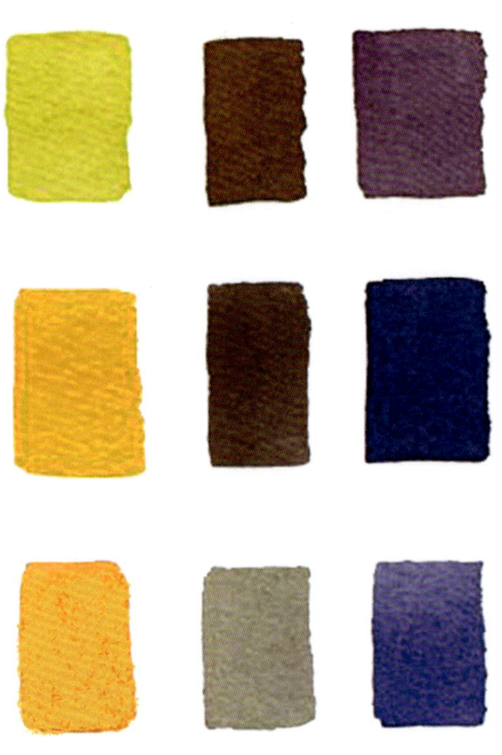

Let's look at more examples of mixed complementary colors.

The yellow and purple examples show the salient impact they have on each other. These mixtures also demonstrate how the less intense colors can vary depending on which yellows (a more *orange*-yellow versus a *green*-yellow) and which purples (a more *red*-purple versus a more *blue*-purple) are mixed.

Take a moment to study these different pairs of yellows and purples, as well as the subsequent mixtures, because your desired brown or sandy color can turn up when yellow and purple dance together.

Notice that these mixed complementary color pairs of yellow and purple resulted in a gray, black, or brown. A true pairing of color complements, or color opposites, mixes into a gray, black, or brown.

I find these mixed, desaturated colors lovely. Once you begin experimenting with your complementary colors, mixing duller hues becomes easier, and your confidence increases. Hopefully you will be surprised by their beauty and be inspired to use them in future paintings.

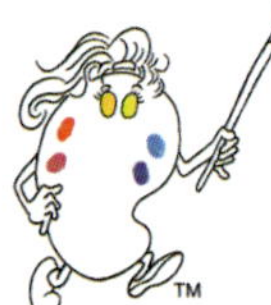

COLOR TIP: A true pair of complementary colors shows no evidence of the hue of either color of the original pair.

In other words, color complements only mix into a gray, black, or brown. If you mix a pair of colors you believe are complementary and get a desaturated green, you know that your beginning pair was NOT a true complementary color pairing.

Continuing with another example, in the next chart, I used the same green but mixed it with two different reds.

See how different this outcome is? The top mixture is a bit browner, whereas the bottom is a black. This happens because the top red is an *orange*-red and the bottom is a *violet*-red even though they are mixed with the same green and are both pairs of complementary colors.

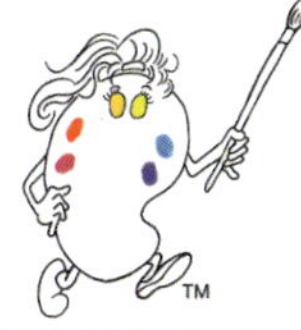

COLOR TIP: Experiment mixing burnt sienna, as your orange, with a range of blues to discover a variety of grays, blacks, and browns.

An excellent exercise for exploring the potential of your complementary colors is to paint what I call a Chromatic Scales Chart. These chromatic scales are perfect for seeing how your complementary colors impact each other.

You also end up with a valuable color mixing reference tool.

Turn the page to get started.

Exercise #5: Chromatic Scales Chart

Step 1: Setting up your chart

Take a piece of 16″ x 12″ canvas or watercolor paper and turn it horizontal. I recommend using the entire sheet for this chart because I have too often run out of space when painting my chromatic scales.

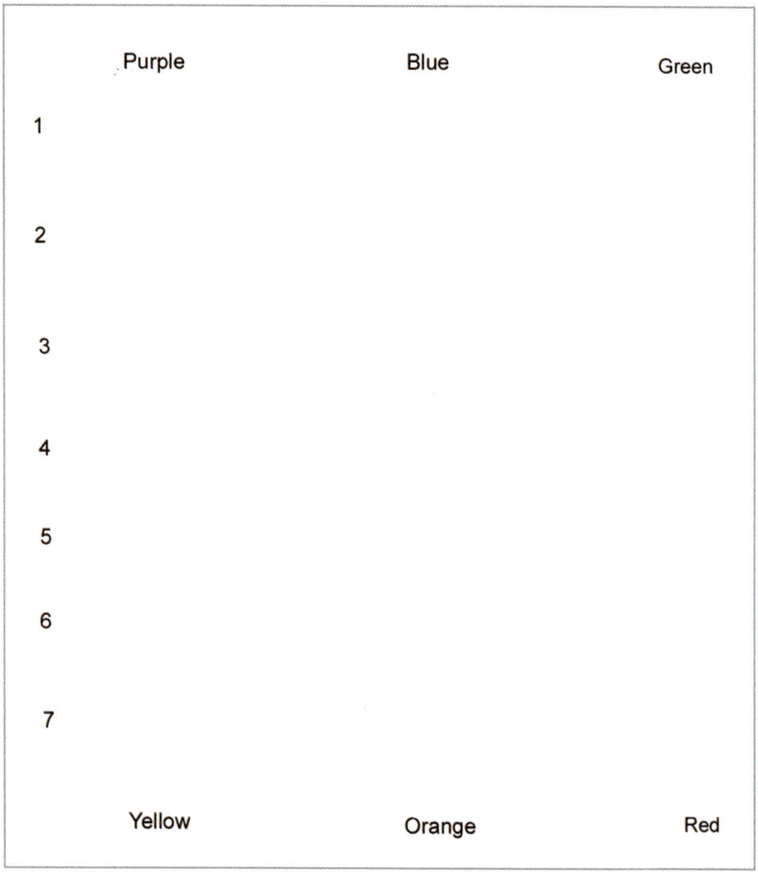

	Purple	Blue	Green
1			
2			
3			
4			
5			
6			
7			
	Yellow	Orange	Red

Step 2: Labeling your complementary pairs and steps

Start by creating three columns, each representing one pair of complementary colors. As you can see here, I labeled these Purple, Blue and Green across the top, and the corresponding Yellow, Orange and Red across the bottom. By the way, you can place your pairs in any sequence that works for you.

Down the left side of the paper, equally space the numbers 1 through 7. These will serve as a guide when painting your swatches of color.

You will be creating three 7-step chromatic scales in this chart.

Step 3: Mixing one pair of complementary colors

Squeeze out (or mix) a good-sized pile of pigment onto your palette for each of the parent, or source, colors for your complementary pairing. You will need to mix your own secondary colors if you do not have tube colors. Remember to label the tube name and brand of the colors you choose.

Paint an approximate 1″ x ½″ swatch of each of the two source colors—a yellow and a purple is used in this example.

Note: I added a small amount of white to each, which is evident on the right side of the swatch. I do this so you can more easily see the color changes in this printed format.

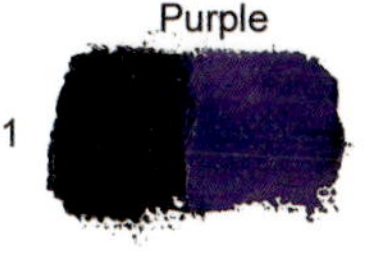

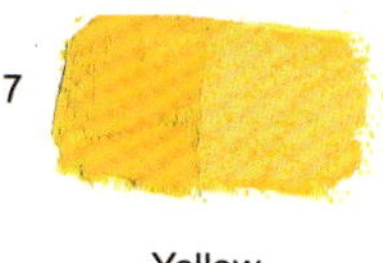

Step 4: Mixing the middle mixture

Next, mix the middle mixture. It will be the *most desaturated color* that can be achieved between the two complementary colors.

When you no longer see either yellow or purple within the mixture, then you have achieved this level of desaturation in the middle mixture.

It takes trial and error to reach this color, so don't give up. You may have to add a little purple, and then some yellow, and then back and forth until you get it. The more you do it, the easier it gets. Once you get the desaturation you want, paint a swatch of this color next to #4.

What's your reaction to this mixture of purple and yellow? Be aware that your mixture may be brown, gray, or black, depending on the yellow and purple you use.

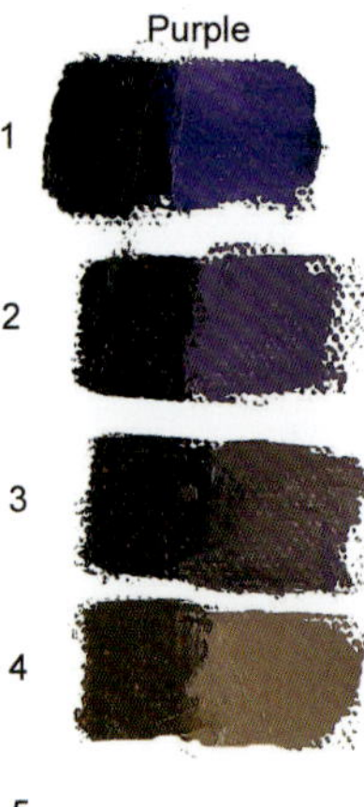

Step 5: Continue mixing the steps in between

For the next mixture, start with your purple and add small amounts of yellow until the hue change is evident. Apply this at #2.

Mix the next swatch by adding more purple, per the example at right. You will see some purple in swatch #2 and #3.

What do you think of these desaturated, or less intense, purples?

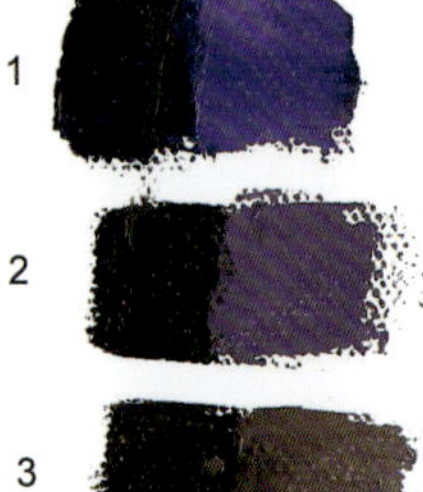

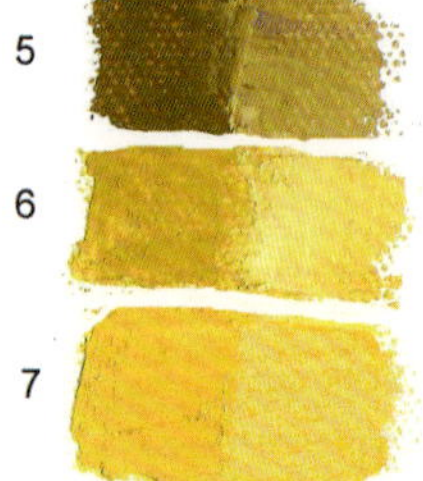

Step 6: Continue mixing the yellow end of the scale

Now, mix the two swatches going in the other direction. Start with the yellow and add just a little bit of purple. Notice how quickly the yellow becomes dull. Apply it at #6.

For the next swatch, add some more purple.

Ta-da! You have completed your first chromatic scale. I call these chromatic scales because the swatches line up like piano keys. Each swatch is unique and incrementally changes in hue from one step to the next, much like a musical scale. In addition, I use the word "chromatic" because in Greek, its root word, "chroma," means color.

Step 7: Mixing your other pairs of complementary colors

Following steps #3 through #6 above, mix a chromatic scale of blue and orange, and then red and green.

Here is my completed chart as a guide.

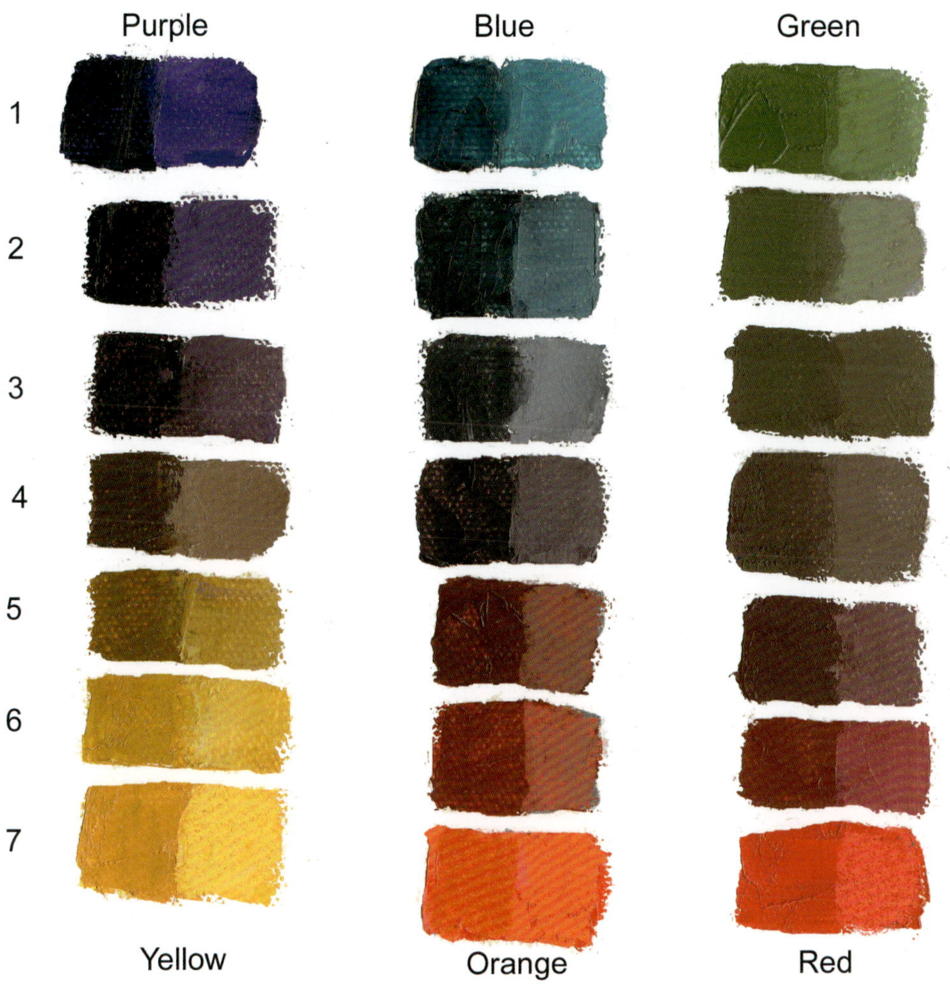

Step 8: Reviewing your completed chart

Take a moment to study your Chromatic Scales Chart. Most likely, you will resonate more with one pair of complementary colors over another. Which pair is it? It is not uncommon to have a favorite pair of complementary colors that you like and a pair you do not care for at all.

In the completed chart on the previous page I have continued to add a little white to the mixtures on the right side of the color swatches. Oil and acrylic painters find this option helpful because it can sometimes be difficult to see the hue of the darker mixtures. It is also nice to see how adding a tiny bit of white impacts the colors. Watercolorists can create a lighter version by adding some water.

Learning how to mix chromatic scales is a color mixing technique that will serve you well throughout your painting career. You won't regret practicing how to do it because mixing any two source colors incrementally helps you find new color combinations that may be the perfect fit for your next painting.

Whenever I want a new color, I'll paint a chromatic scale on a scratch piece of paper. I do this often. My students have said this is one of the most enlightening and beneficial color exercises I ask them to do. In fact, we'll do this again in chapter 7.

This chart shows you a 5-step method of more chromatic scales in watercolors.

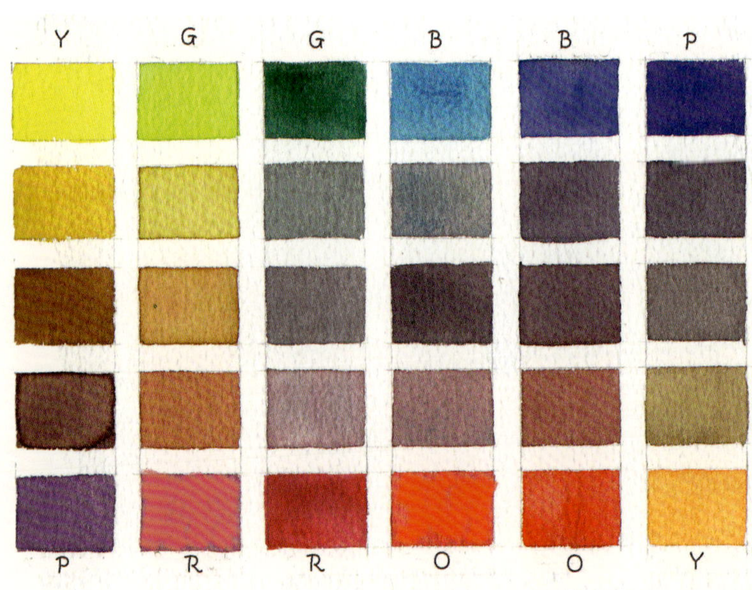

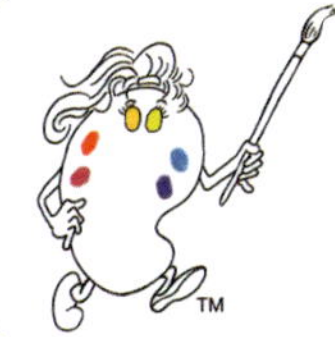

COLOR TIP: Each additional step in your Chromatic Scales Chart will give you more information. Believe it or not, some of my students have painted 9-step chromatic scales.

Congratulations! You have just learned how to mix mud!

Except now, since "mud" usually implies something is wrong with the color, you don't need to call these "mud" anymore. Instead, these have become delightful, desaturated colors ready for your next painting.

Just in case you need more inspiration, here are more chromatic scales, working with acrylic paints. Each swatch has a little water added to it to show a thinner variation of the color.

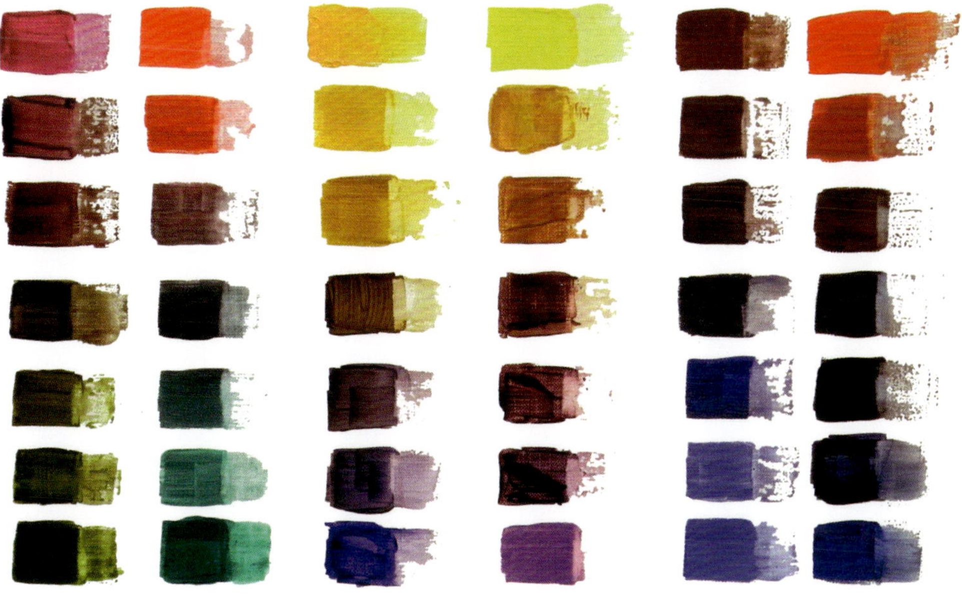

The more you study and work with any pair of complementary colors, the more you will see how an entire painting can be painted with only two colors. Look online, or visit art shows, to find paintings that exemplify this. Reflect on how you respond to them.

Here is an example of one of my paintings using orange and blue and the various desaturated colors in between.

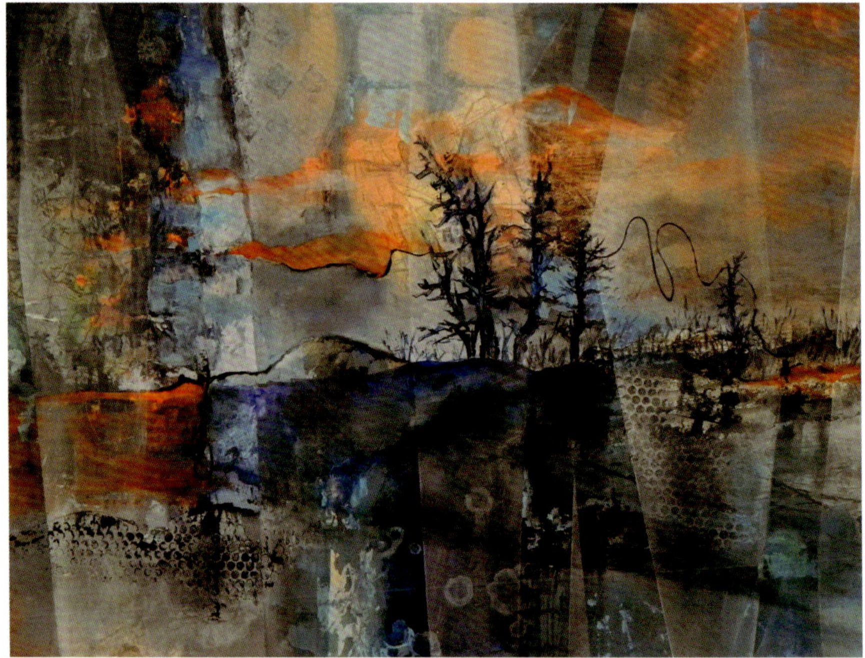

Out on the Prairie, mixed media on board, 18″ x 24.″

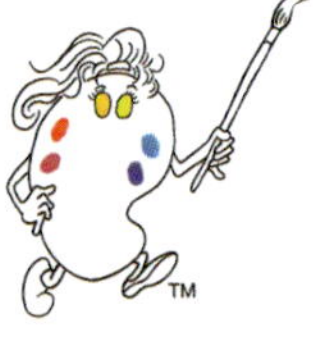

COLOR TIP: When three or more tubes of paint are mixed, the chances of mixing mud increases significantly because there is a high possibility that a pair of complementary colors is carried within those three colors. Your knowledge about color bias and complementary colors, will decrease your tendency to play in muddy waters.

Value: As It Relates to Complementary Colors

As mentioned in chapter 2, value refers to the *light to dark* scale of a color. These value scales can typically be seen in five, seven, or nine steps. Below is a 9-step value scale, with 1 representing white, 9 representing black, and the gradations of gray in equal steps in between. You will sometimes see value scales that run from 0 to 9, and some variation thereof, including value scales where 9 is white and 1 is black. There is no standard per se, yet it is important to know about value scales and how to use them. As mentioned, the latter will not be discussed in this book.

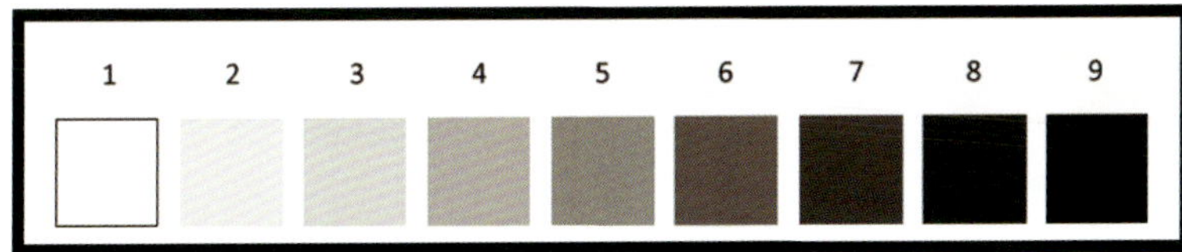

As you painted your Chromatic Scales Chart, you probably noticed the mixtures—the yellows and the purples—simultaneously changed in saturation *and* value. In other words, they became duller *and* darker.

Here is a chromatic scale of yellow and purple turned horizontally so you can more easily compare it to the above value scale.

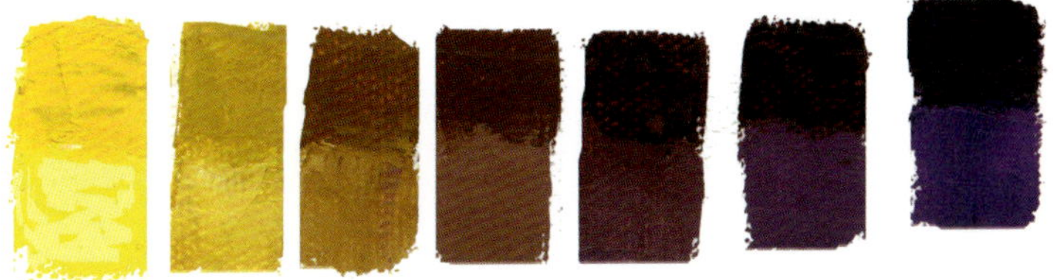

Observe how the values become darker from left to right. Seeing the value of color is a useful skill when you want to create contrast in your painting.

Many articles, painting classes, videos, and art instruction books discuss the importance of understanding values. I encourage you to study these resources as you develop your painting skills because we do not go into this very important color concept in this book.

Another benefit of mixing paints for your Chromatic Scales Chart is the discovery of dark hues. Painters often complain that they don't know how to mix darks, and they resort to adding tube black to a mixture. But adding tube black deadens your color mixture; it has no life in it. Mixing black with a color also changes the integrity of the original hue more than desired.

Mixing your own darks, without using tube black, will enliven your paintings with color richness and potential contrasts. Go back and take a look at the darks you created on your Chromatic Scales Chart and decide for yourself.

Complementary Colors Expanded

Until now, I have referred to complementary colors found on a 6-hue color wheel.

To find, and experiment, with more dancing partners, refer to this 12-hue color wheel.

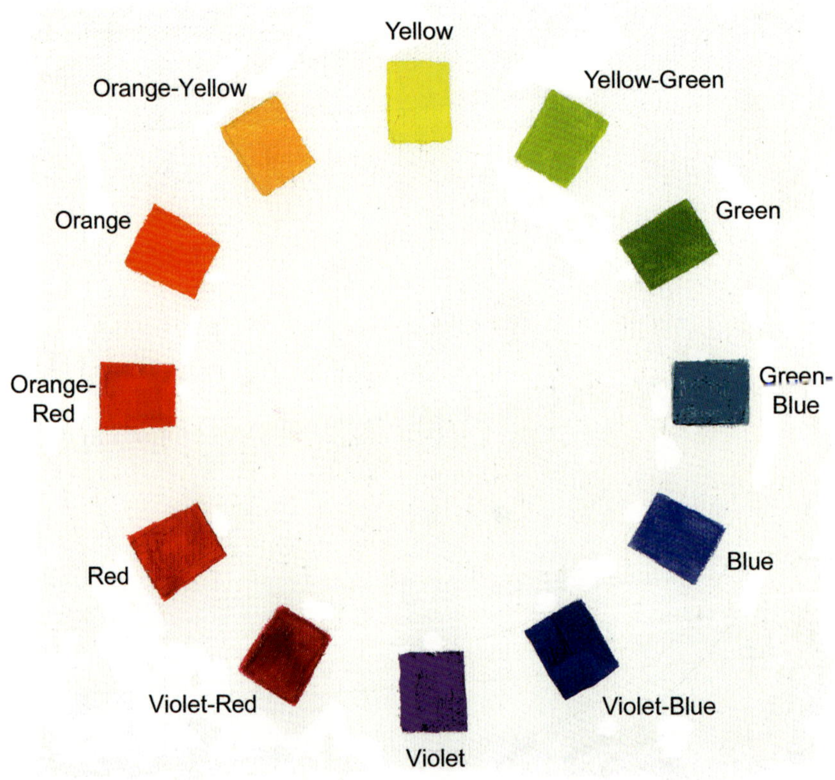

Pick one color and then go across the wheel to find its dancing partner. A pair that is not well known and rarely used in paintings is that of a *violet*-red with a *yellow*-green.

Try this pairing, and perhaps another pair you have never considered, and paint a chromatic scale of these. It's a wonderful way to expand your color mixing knowledge, explore the infinite potential of color, and discover a foundation of self-assurance as an artist.

I call complementary colors dancing partners because they work well together in a variety of ways. The more you know about them, the easier it becomes when it's time to mix and apply them in your paintings.

Questions to Ponder

- What discoveries did you make about complementary colors?
- Did you find any darks that you liked?
- Were there any surprises? If so, what were they?
- Which pair of color opposites seemed to resonate with you?
- Did you see how a painting could work with a single pair of complementary colors and still be all you wanted it to be? (Note: Acrylic and oil painters can add white. Watercolorists can add water.)

Now that you know how complementary colors impact each other when mixed, in the next chapter we're going to add the impact of *color bias* to your color mixing skills. The real secret to mixing clean colors, or intentionally mixing desaturated (aka "mud") colors when you want them, lies within these two core color mixing concepts—**color bias** and **complementary colors**. We are going to put this knowledge into play immediately as we mix bright and dull secondary colors.

Notes

CHAPTER 5

How to Mix Bright and Dull Secondaries

Love mixing those greens, purples, and oranges!

Have you ever been exasperated trying to mix a bright purple? You have been told since you were a youngster that red and blue make purple, right? Yet experience has proven otherwise. I remember mixing what I thought was a red and blue, but the result was not purple. Then you try to mix a bright green and get something less than bright.

Then you go out and buy tubes of purples and greens, and they also are unsatisfactory. Why is this?

In the last chapter, you discovered how pairs of complementary colors impact each other and how quickly this happens. Even a small amount of a complementary color immediately changes the hue of a parent color.

Now we can combine what you learned about complementary color mixtures with your knowledge of color bias. The road merges here as the magic of the Balanced Palette System comes into play. It isn't really magic, though when I learned it and started to use it, it felt like magic.

The secret is learning *how* to use a balanced palette. Many art instructors talk about having two colors for each primary on their palettes—a warm and a cool of each—but they do not show you how to mix these while maximizing their potential.

Once you start mixing from this palette, you will see how you can mix almost any color with your six colors—plus white if you use an opaque medium such as oils, acrylics, water mixable oils, and acrylics.

The simplicity, clarity, and power of the Balanced Palette System makes color mixing achievable and fun. It is also a straightforward approach when you want to mix bright and dull secondaries.

Reviewing your balanced palette

Remember, the balanced palette is based on strategically choosing six primary colors—two yellows, two reds, and two blues. Each of these primaries needs to carry a strong color bias.

With your yellows, you want an obvious color bias of green and orange, or a *green*-yellow and an *orange*-yellow.

For your blues, you want one that carries a strong *green*-blue and the other with a strong *violet*-blue.

And for the reds, you want an obvious *violet*-red and an obvious *orange*-red. Now, let's put this Balanced Palette System to work and mix some bright *and* dull greens, purples, and oranges.

Exercise #6: Mixing Bright and Dull Secondary Colors

As you learn to mix secondaries, you will see why you will not need to own so many tubes of greens, purples, or oranges.

Step 1: Setting up your chart

First, grab your Balanced Palette Color Chart from chapter 3. Do you remember how we left the bottom half of that chart empty? With a ruler, draw two rows similar to those below and then draw in three equal columns.

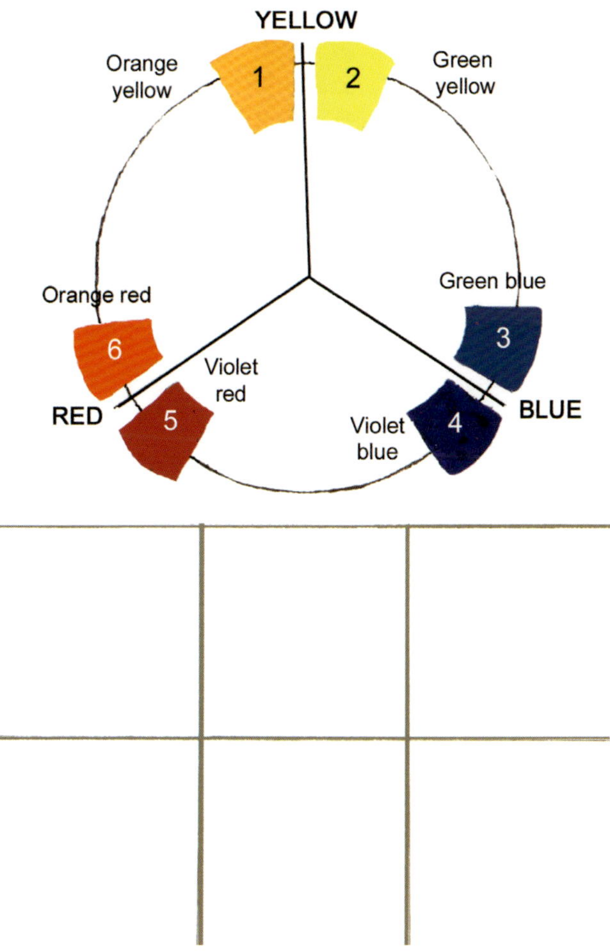

Step 2: Labeling your grid

Across the top row, we will be mixing bright or saturated secondaries, and the second row will contain dull or desaturated secondaries. Label them as I have here.

Next, label the columns across the top corresponding to the three secondary colors—green, purple, and orange.

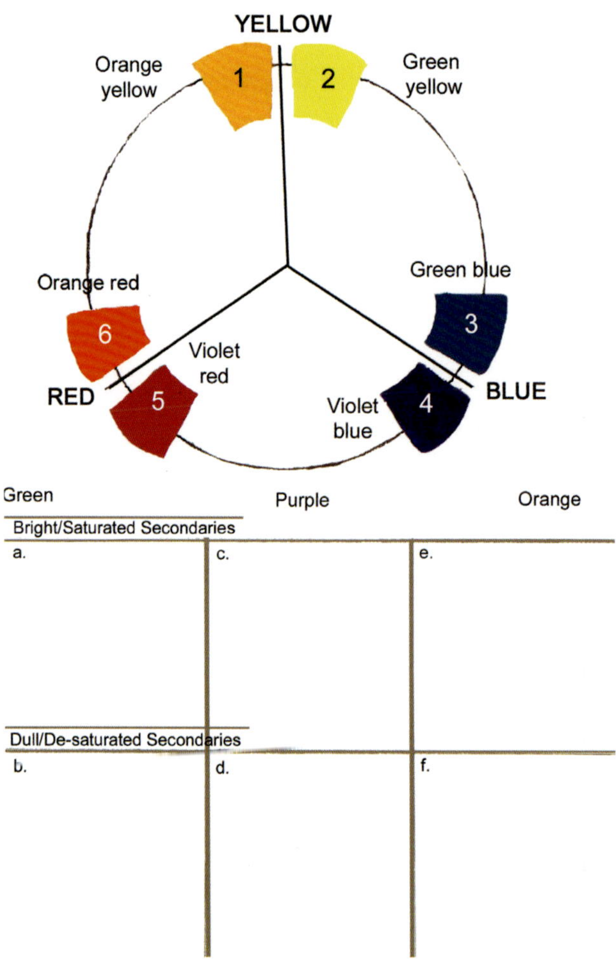

Now, label each box from "a" to "f," following the sequence here.

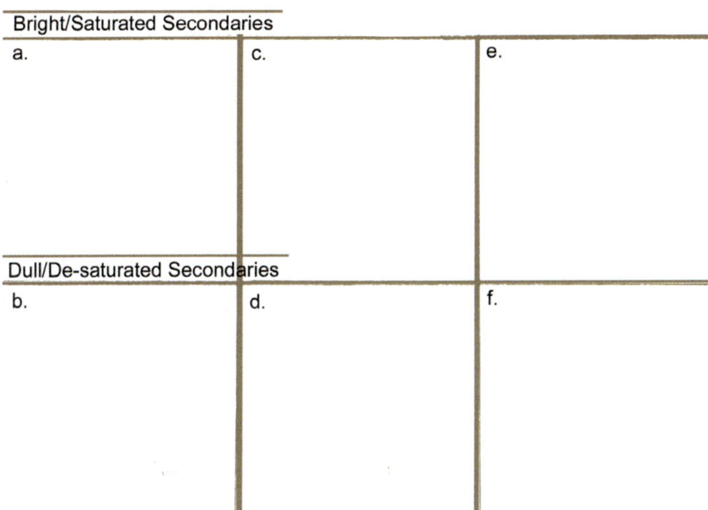

Step 3: Mixing a bright and a dull green

This is when the numbering of your Balanced Palette Color Wheel comes into play. I will be referring to the six numbers of the six primaries throughout the creation of this new chart.

Step 3-i: To mix a bright green, you will need your *green*-yellow (#2) and your *green*-blue (#3). Why this yellow and blue? Because neither one of these yellow or blue primaries carries a red bias in it. Notice that the adjective, or color bias, of these two primary colors is "green." Refer to the modified Balanced Palette Color Wheel at right to further understand.

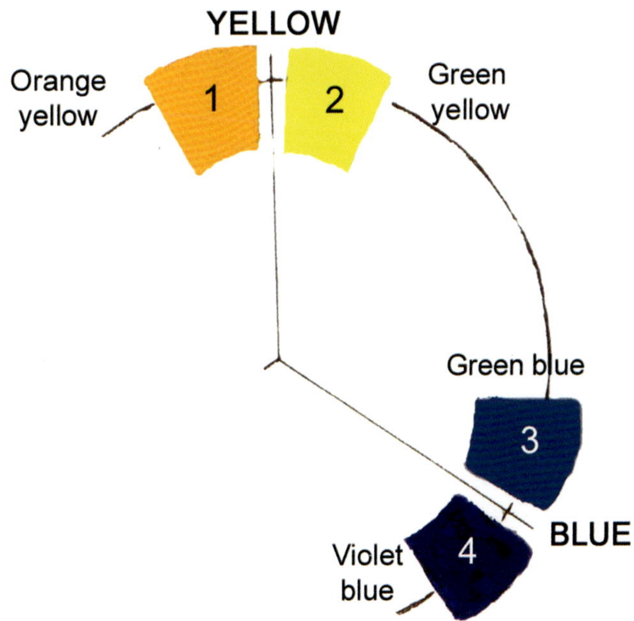

Step 3-ii: Before you mix this yellow and blue, paint a swatch of each parent color in the upper left-hand box, labeled "a," as I have done here. Now mix these two and apply the bright green in between them.

It may be helpful to reference the completed chart on page 71.

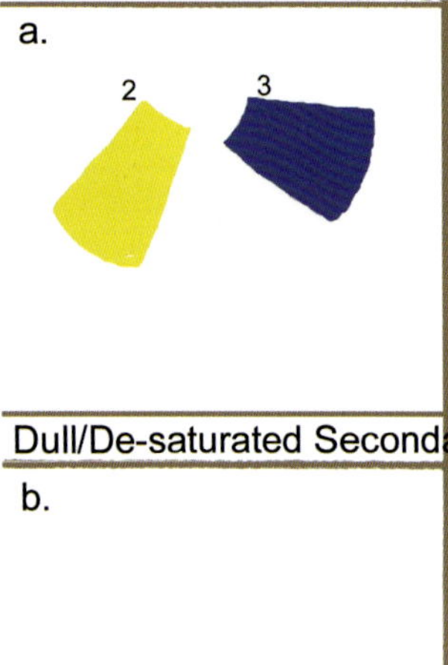

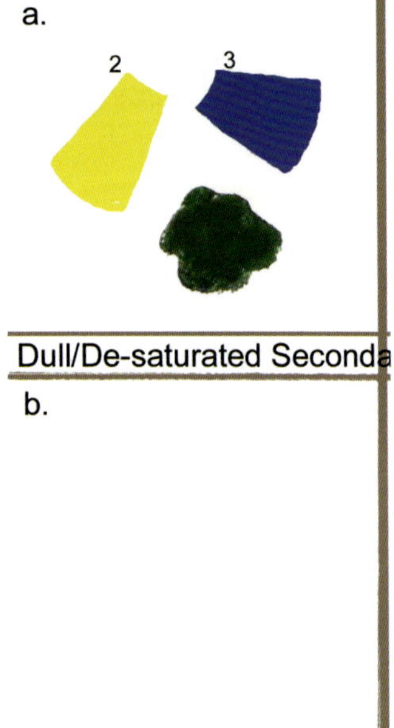

Step 3-iii: To mix a dull green, grab your *orange*-yellow (#1) and *violet*-blue (#4). Again, refer to the color wheel on page 63 to see where they are located on the balanced palette. Paint swatches of them into the box labeled "b." Then mix them and apply this swatch in between the parent colors as you did for your bright green.

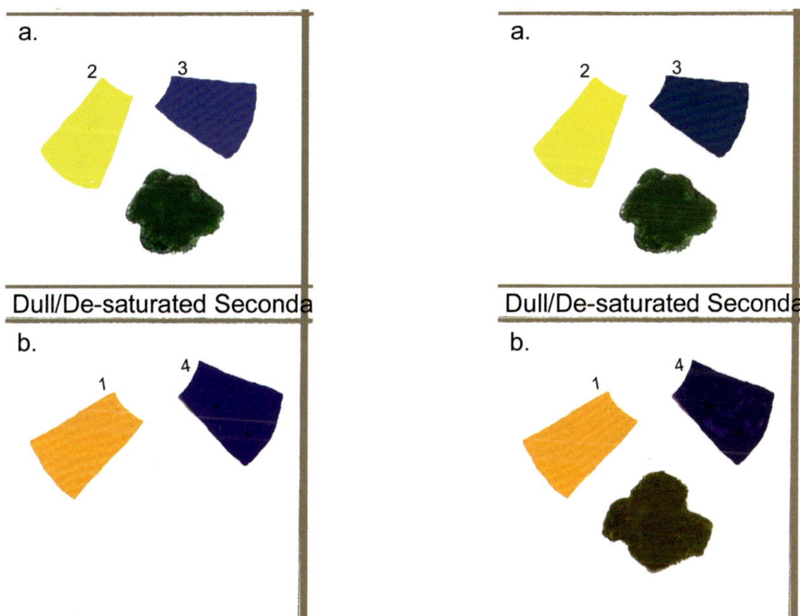

Both of these primaries carry a red color bias in them. You know from your mixing with complementary colors that red and green, when mixed, desaturate each other. Hence, this mixture of *orange*-yellow with *violet*-blue results in a dull green.

Now you have experienced the relationship between identifying the color bias of primary colors and the impact of complementary colors! You are also learning how to use the Balanced Palette System and its effectiveness.

Isn't this cool? When I first started using this approach to mixing secondary colors, clarity emerged! I was jazzed and very excited. In chapter 7, we'll expand upon mixing greens even more.

Step 4: Mixing a bright and dull purple

Step 4-i: To mix a bright purple, look at the modified Balanced Palette Color Wheel below. Given what you learned about mixing a bright green, you can surmise that a bright purple will result when mixing a *violet*-blue (#4) with and *violet*-red (#5). Both of these primaries carry a color bias of violet; hence they are not influenced by yellow—the complement of purple.

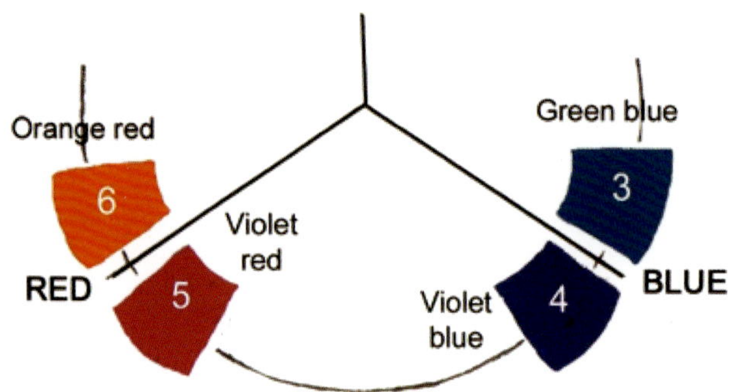

Step 4-ii: In the box labeled "c," paint a swatch of your *violet*-blue (#4) and your *violet*-red (#5). Next, mix these two and paint a swatch of the purple mixture in between. In the swatch below, you can see that the mixture of #5 with #4 is a bright purple.

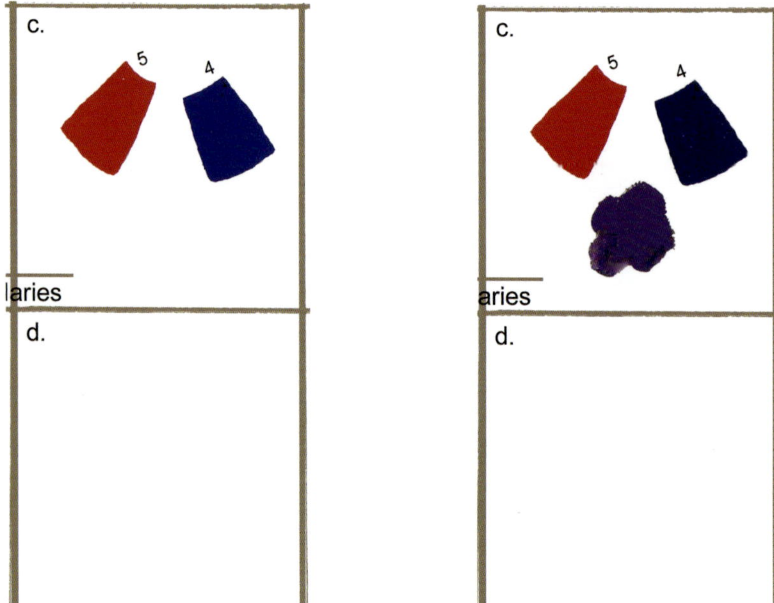

Now let's discover what happens when you mix your *orange*-red (#3) with your *green*-blue (#6).

They both have a color bias of yellow, which is the complement of purple. Hence the resulting mixing is going to be dull, or desaturated.

Collect your *orange*-red and your *green*-blue tubes of paint. Paint a swatch of each in the box labeled "d." Next, mix them and paint the resulting mixture. Interestingly, this mixture usually produces a dark *purple*-black, as you can see in this example. In other words, purple is barely evident.

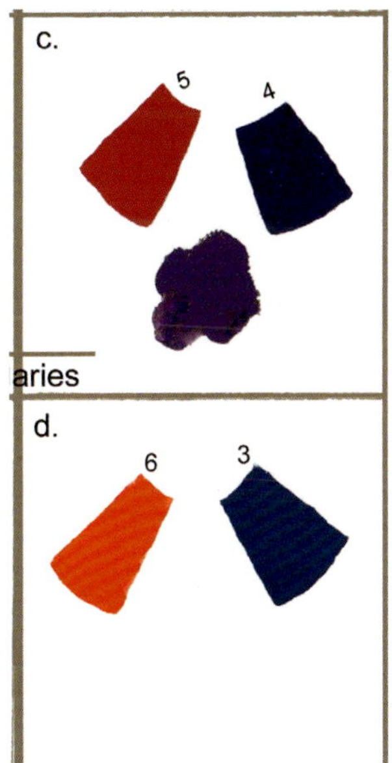

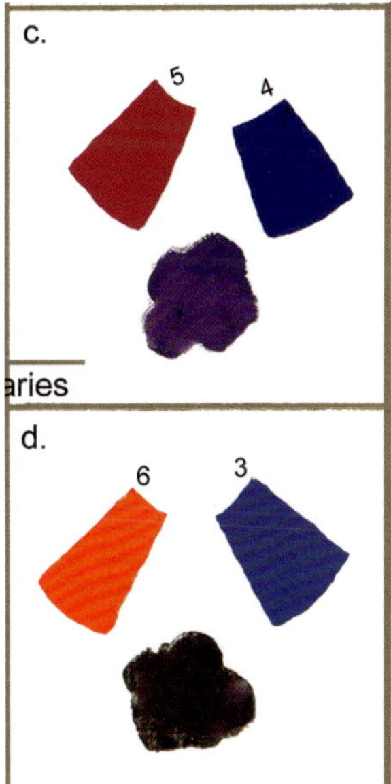

And this is why "red and blue" do not always make purple!

COLOR TIP: If your *violet*-red is alizarin crimson, the resulting purple will not be bright.

The hue in alizarin crimson is slightly desaturated. Hence it will not mix into a bright or saturated purple. If you want brighter purples, try a permanent rose, thalo red, or magenta for your *violet*-red.

Step 5: Mixing a bright orange and a dull orange

Many painters don't typically concern themselves with learning how to mix bright and dull oranges. We just dip our brush into a yellow and a red, all the while accepting whatever orange is mixed.

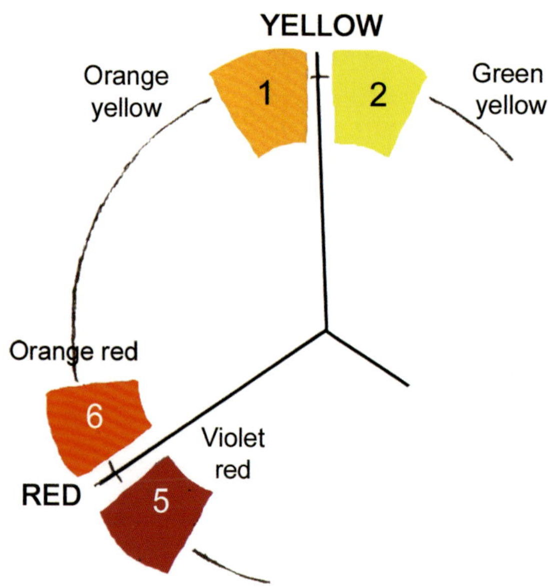

Referring to this modified Balanced Palette Color Wheel, let's use your new knowledge to expand your options for the next time you need orange in your painting.

Step 5-i: To mix a bright orange, you need your *orange*-red (#6) and your *orange*-yellow (#1). Notice that each of these primaries has an orange or red color bias. The color complement of blue is not carried in either of them. Paint the parent color swatches into box "e." Next mix the two and paint a swatch of the bright orange in between.

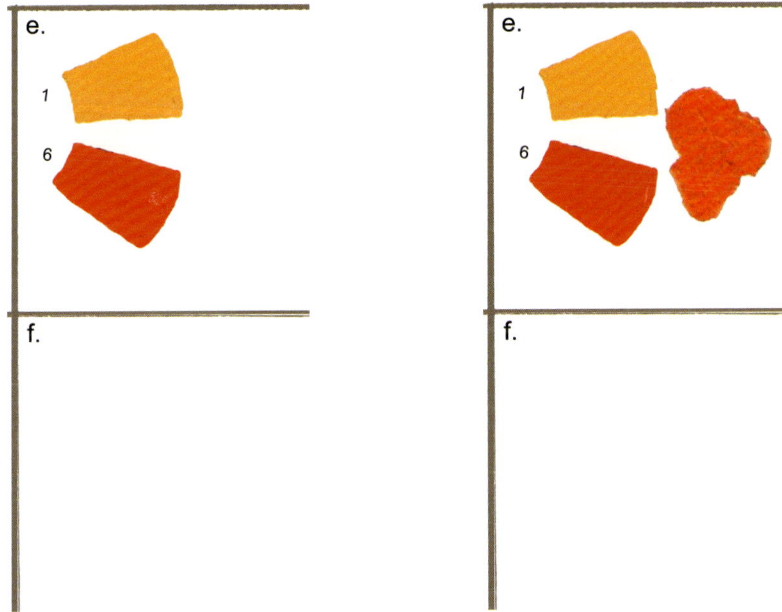

Step 5-ii: To mix a dull orange, you need your *violet*-red (#5) and your *green*-yellow (#2). Each of these primary colors carries some blue in it. Since orange and blue are complements, they will dull the orange mixture. Paint a swatch of each parent color into the box labeled "f." Next, mix them and apply the swatch of dull orange in between.

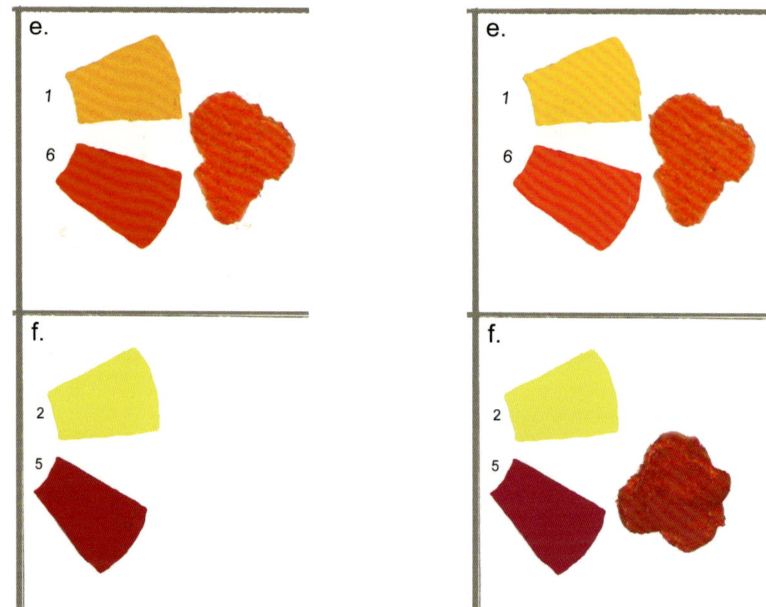

Can you see yourself applying this knowledge of bright and dull oranges the next time you paint a pumpkin, an orange cloth, or a fall landscape? The brighter orange could be used on the sun, or light, side of an object, and the duller orange on the shadow side.

Step 6. Reviewing your *Mixing Bright and Dull Secondary Colors Chart*

Creating a chart of your bright and dull color mixtures gives you an excellent reference as you move through the next chapters. Hopefully you will find, as I did years ago, how liberating this approach to mixing color is. The assurance I acquired when mixing bright or dull secondary colors was invaluable. Keep this chart handy as a reference, and a reminder, when you want to mix dull or bright secondary colors.

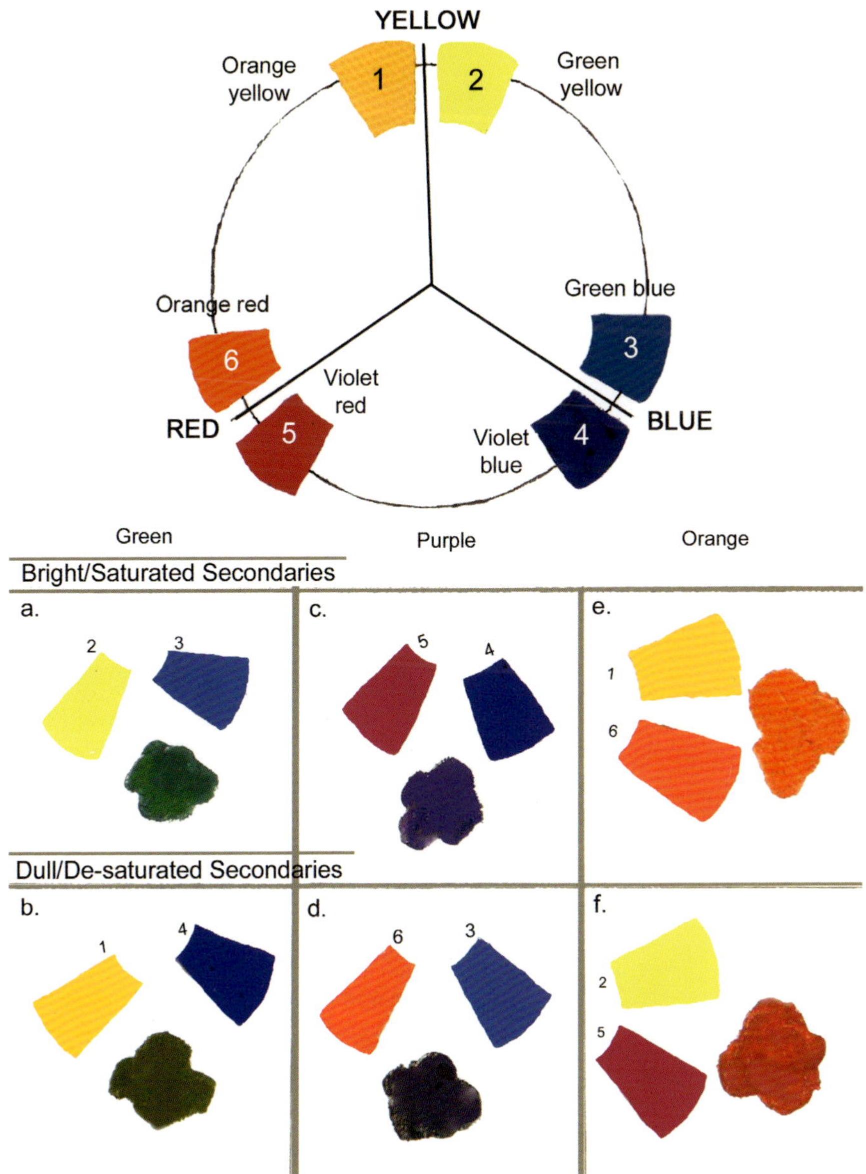

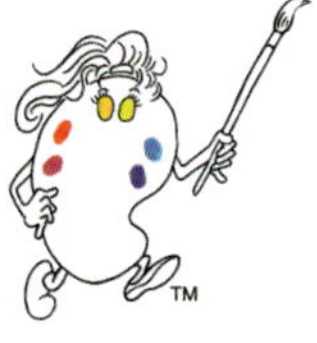

COLOR TIP: If you have trouble identifying a blue's color bias, mix it with a clean *violet*-red. If you get a nice bright purple, then that blue is a *violet*-blue. If you get a dullish purple, then your blue is a *green*-blue.

You can use this same technique to identify the color bias of your reds and yellows.

If you still can't identify the color bias of a yellow, red, or blue, leave it alone for now. Once you learn to mix with a balanced palette, you can return to solve this problem.

When you intentionally mix one color with another that has a color bias of its complementary color, you can expect a resulting duller color. As you have seen and experienced, dull colors can be desirable and lovely. It's just more pleasant when you have control over them. On the flip side, it's quite delightful when you know exactly how to mix bright secondaries.

Questions to Ponder

- What surprised you the most after mixing your bright and dull secondaries?
- Do you see why you don't need to own tubes of purple, green, or orange?
- Is the role that color bias plays in mixing colors clear to you?

Are you ready to take your knowledge of the Balanced Palette System to the next level and learn more ways to mix intentional mud? Let's check out chapter 6.

CHAPTER 6

Prevent Mixing Mud #2: Why Tertiary Colors Matter

Mix beautiful muddy colors intentionally

Let's mix mud. Really?
You might be thinking, *I do this all the time!*

But what if you knew the various ways to deliberately make mud so you could avoid it when you wanted? Or use it where you wanted?

In chapter 4, you learned how to mix desaturated colors by using complementary colors. Some painters call these "muddy" colors because 1) they have lost their saturation and 2) painters accidently mix desaturated colors when they want something else.

In this chapter, we are going into a specific method for mixing desaturated colors (aka "mud") by learning how to mix tertiary colors. Unfortunately, the definition of *tertiary* is not agreed upon across the painting world. Many color instructors define a tertiary color as the hue between a secondary and primary color. This is not correct, which is regrettable because…

This incorrect definition stops painters from learning how to mix tertiary colors, which, in turn, prevents them from maximizing the potential of their paints.

Logically, if a secondary color is created by mixing two primary colors, then **a tertiary color is created by mixing two secondary colors**.

Tertiaries are created when you mix two secondary colors:

- Orange with green
- Green with purple
- Purple with orange

Let's discover what happens when we mix our secondary colors. I believe you will be pleasantly surprised.

Looking at the images below, see if you can answer the questions. Guess if necessary. When I posted this image and question on Facebook, most people were not able to answer correctly, or they said, "Mud."

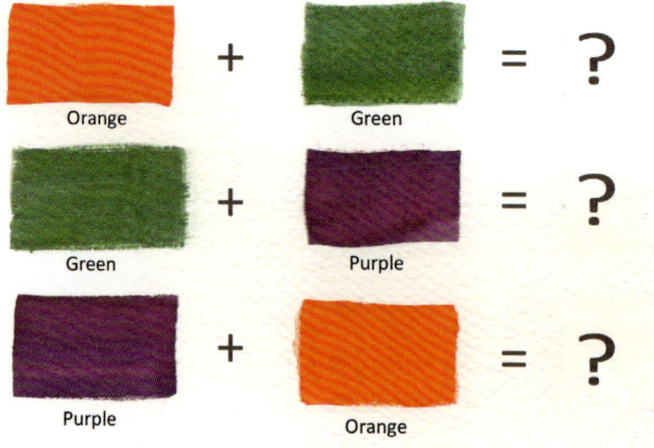

In the next image, take a look at the results from mixing these secondaries using watercolors.

- The purple and green mix into a blue-gray, or slate, color.
- When green and orange are mixed, a rich olive green is achieved.
- Perhaps one interesting surprise is seeing the results of mixing purple and orange because they mix into a rich burnt sienna.

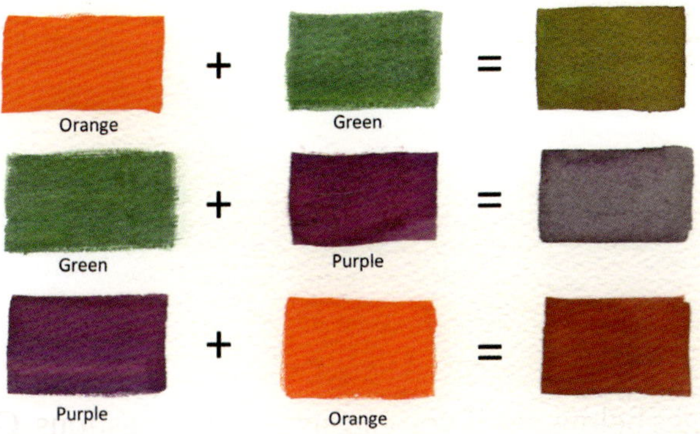

Exercise #7: Mixing Tertiary Colors

This chart is an effective way to learn about tertiary colors.

Step 1: Setting up your grid

To begin, use a piece of canvas paper or watercolor paper of approximately 12″ x 6″ turned vertically. With a clear 18″ ruler and pencil, draw out a grid similar to the one below, which has three columns and nine rows.

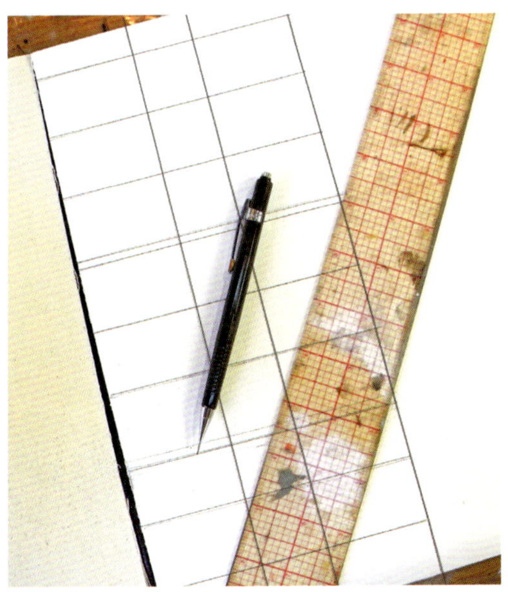

Since you will be mixing the three different tertiary combinations, draw a double line to separate these into three sections. Each row is about 1¼″ deep to allow plenty of room for applying swatches of color.

The top section is for mixing oranges with purples, the next section for mixing greens with oranges, and the last for mixing purples with oranges. It might be helpful to label these sections as I have displayed here.

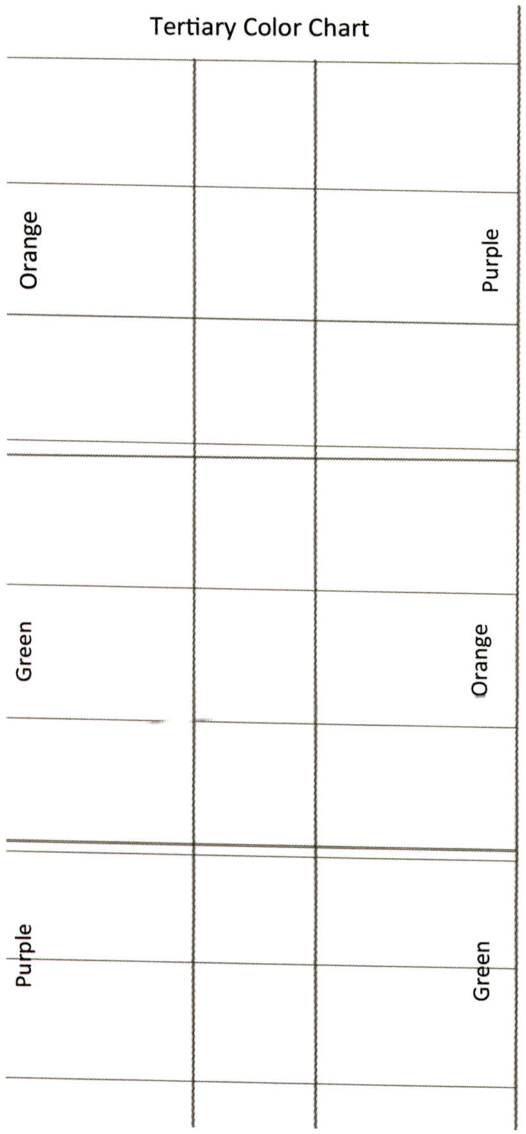

Tertiary Color Chart

Orange

Purple

Green

Orange

Purple

Green

Step 2: Painting your swatches of orange and purple

As you paint your swatches, remember to write down the paints you use under each swatch.

From your knowledge of mixing secondary colors in chapter 4, first mix a pile of bright orange.

Next, apply two swatches of orange in the top two rows, as seen here. I suggest that you use the same orange, but mix with two different purples so that you can experience the slightly different results.

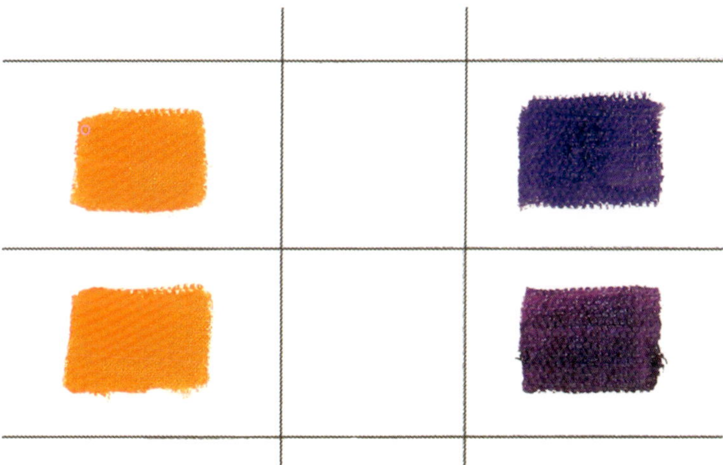

Then mix two different purples—one a *blue*-violet and one a *red*-violet. You can also use tube colors of orange and purple for this exercise.

Paint the purple swatches in the right sections of the grid as seen above.

Step 3: Mixing your orange with your purple

Now, mix your two combinations of orange and purple. Then apply this mixture in the middle between the corresponding orange and purple.

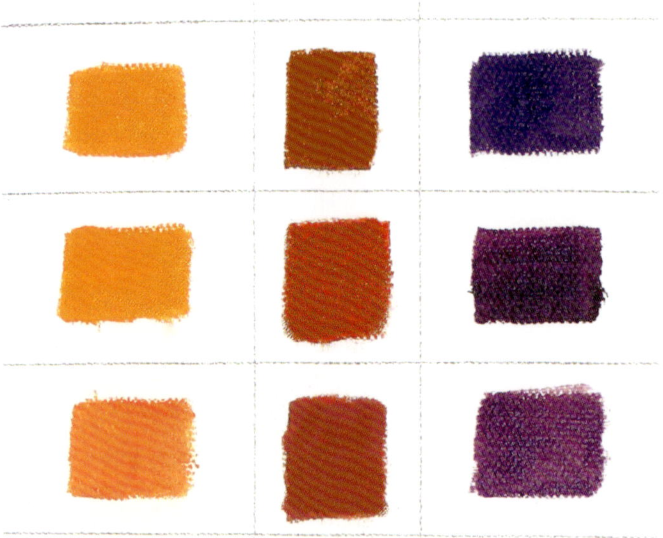

The result will be a variation of burnt sienna!

In this example, I added a third row of colors. The orange is a duller hue, and I mixed it with a redder purple. Experimenting with variations of colors is both revealing and exciting.

The more you play around with your colors, the more you can discover their potential. It's not unlike taking a road trip into unknown territory and discovering a glorious vista around the bend that you had not expected.

I remember being in a watercolor workshop when an instructor asked if we knew how to mix burnt sienna. The room was awkwardly silent. We were dumbfounded when she demonstrated how mixing orange and purple created rich burnt sienna hues. She went on to say that she never bought tubes of burnt sienna.

Step 4: Continue mixing tertiary color combinations

As per the completed chart below and following the steps above, mix your tertiary color combinations of orange with green, and green with purple.

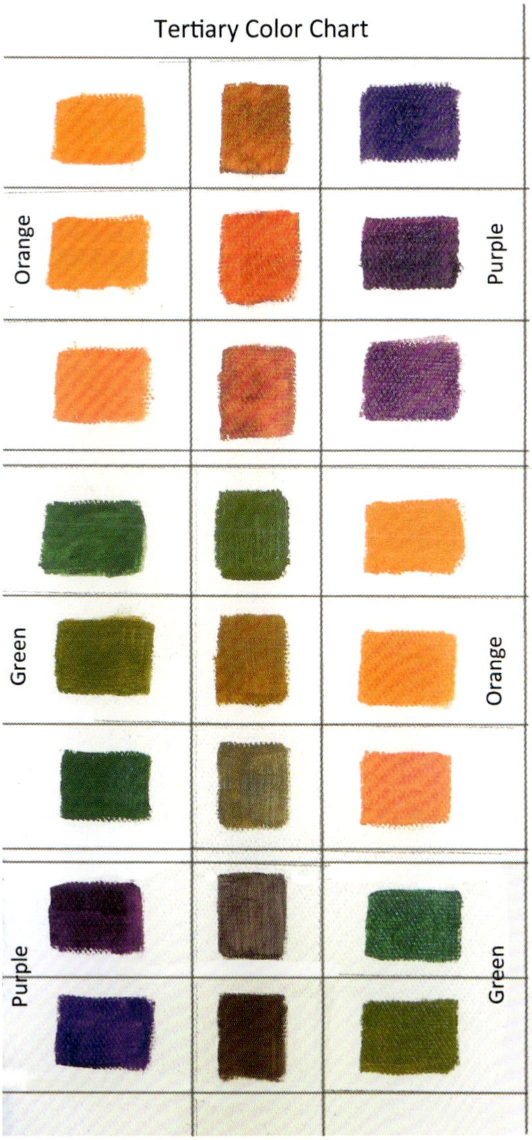

Tertiary Color Chart

Orange Purple

Green Orange

Purple Green

You can see in the second section, where I mixed greens with oranges, that I varied the green mixtures, one being a *blue*-green and the other a more *yellow*-green. Again, this shows how the results can differ slightly.

Step 5: Reviewing your tertiary chart

Take a moment to review your column of tertiaries. Do any of them look like the "mud" you may have mixed in paintings when you didn't want to? Now you know how these dull, or desaturated, colors can show up. All of these tertiary colors are legitimate. Scan your interior and exterior environments, and you will find them. Perhaps noticing them in your surroundings will inspire you to use them in a future painting.

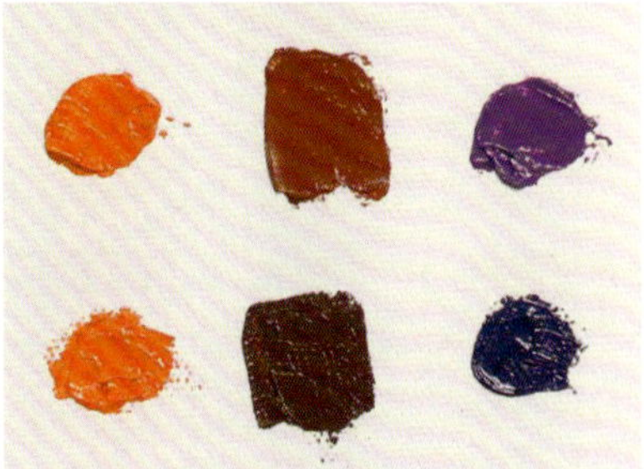

Experiment with your tertiary mixtures. Feel free to design your color chart according to how it best suits you.

Note: The hues of your tertiaries will most likely not be exactly the same as mine. For example, because I used a different set of oil paints, this small chart above shows how these burnt siennas are slightly different from the previous chart.

Here are samples of burnt sienna coming out of paint tubes. Compare them with your mixed burnt sienna. The next time you think you need to buy a tube, you might remember that you can mix your own!

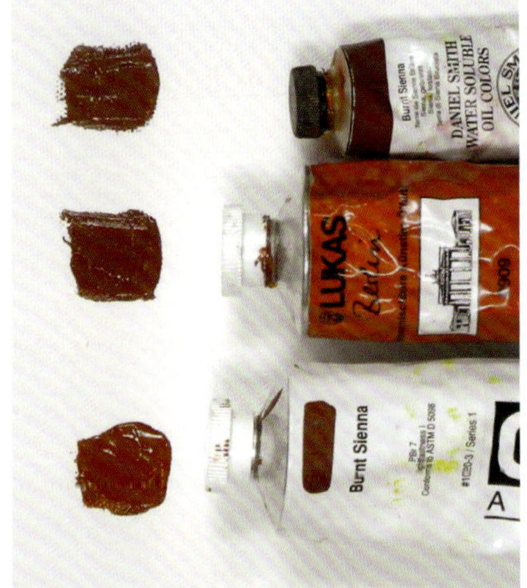

Isn't it eye-opening to see the burnt sienna, olive green, and blue-gray mixtures from these mixed secondaries, also known as tertiaries? As you can see, you don't need to own *a tube* of sap green or burnt sienna because you can make your own—and in a variety no tube can match!

Examples of Applying Tertiary Colors in Paintings

I know this book is focused on mixing color, but I couldn't resist showing how I applied my knowledge of tertiaries to a few of my paintings.

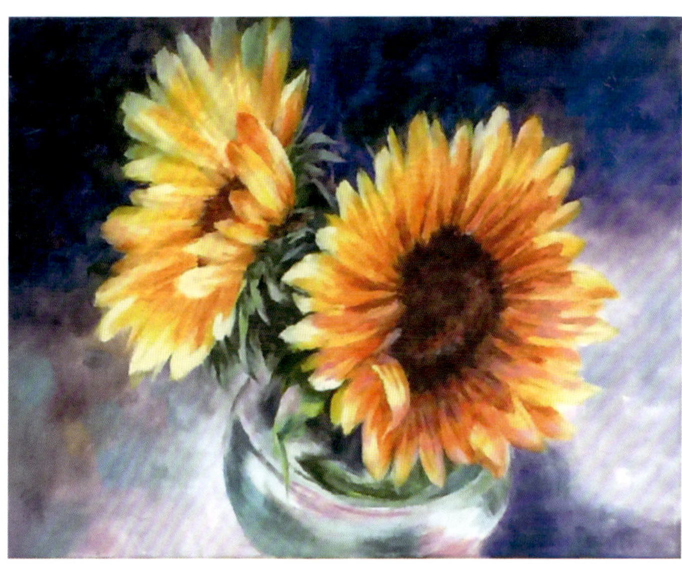

Sunburst, oil on canvas, 8" x 10"

As a resident of the American Southwest, when painting the red rocks of the area or pumpkins, I prefer to dull my oranges by using my purples. I also allow some of the pure oranges and purples to appear in the painting to make it more visually interesting and colorful. This is one way to apply a variety of color in a painting.

Another potential subject for applying purple and orange is the center of a sunflower, as seen here. I did not use any burnt sienna from a tube. Instead, I either mixed it on my palette, stippled the oranges and purples, or layered them.

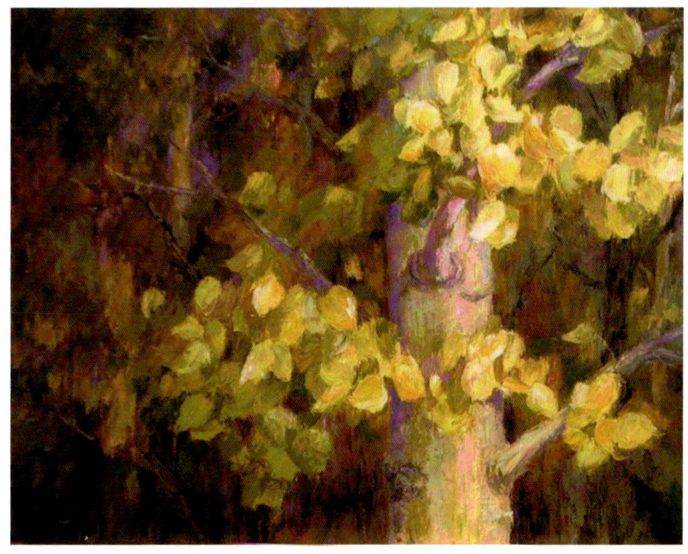

Aspen Dance, oil on canvas, 11" x 14"

My knowledge and love of mixing tertiary colors is on display in this painting of aspen leaves, *Aspen Dance*. There are a variety of mixed burnt siennas in the background.

Below is an example of a pet portrait of my dog, Kyla. Again, I did not use any burnt sienna from a tube. There are highlights of purple and orange throughout. For the initial layers, as seen in Phase 1, I applied different purples to establish the darks. In the second phase, I started adding various oranges. In the last stages of painting, as displayed in Phase 3, I went back and forth with oranges and purples.

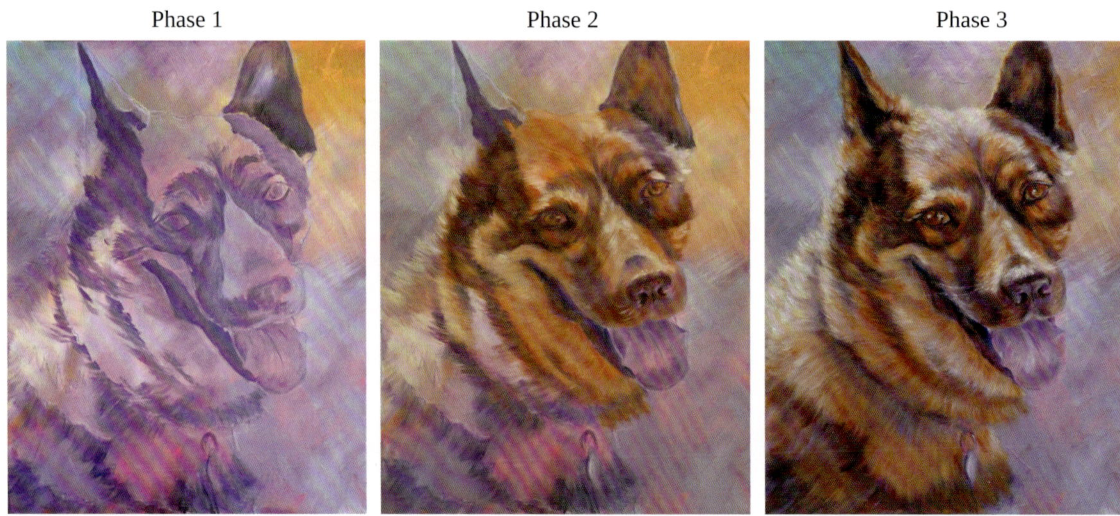
Phase 1 Phase 2 Phase 3

Tertiary colors can also be applied when painting a landscape or foliage. Often, you want a warmer or duller green for these subjects. All you need to do is add some orange to your green, and bingo!—you have lovely olive greens.

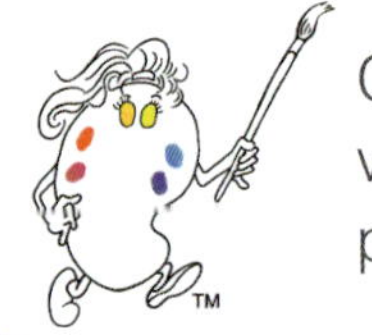

COLOR TIP: Paintings convey a stronger sense of visual unity when you mix with tubes of paint you already have on your palette instead of introducing another tube of paint.

Next, if you want to dull down a green or a purple, instead of mixing its complementary color, add purple to the green and vice versa.

In my painting *Iris Lady*, the blue-gray you see in the background is a tertiary mixture, not a tube color. I frequently use the mixed tertiaries of purple and green when painting flowers or green landscapes. This blue-gray mixture achieves greater color unity because it's mixed from the green and purple I've already applied in the painting. I am also mixing only from my balanced palette—my strategically chosen primaries plus white.

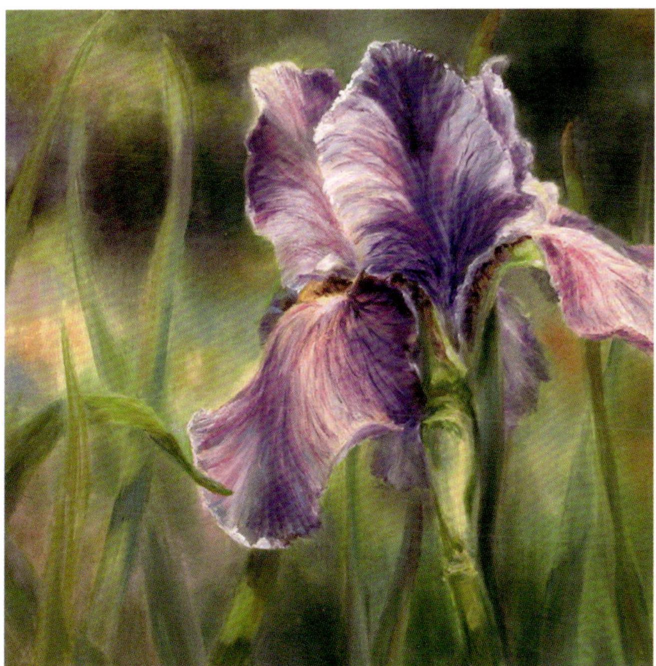

Iris Lady, acrylic on canvas, 10" x 10"

Color decision-making becomes more efficient and expedient once you know what happens when you have a mix of green and purple, orange and purple, or green and orange.

Mixing also becomes easier because you have fewer tubes of paint to consider. Any sense of being overwhelmed decreases, while color confidence increases because mixing is no longer an accident. Or, if an accident occurs, now you know about the impact of mixing secondary colors, and you can determine what went wrong.

Remember, most paintings need desaturated colors to give the viewer's eye a place to rest. When a painting only contains saturated colors, viewers can feel as if the colors are screaming. Now you have a foundation from which to explore these desaturated hues with very few tubes of paint. Find the mixtures of color opposites and tertiary colors that resonate with you and your visual voice.

Questions to Ponder

- Where do you see applying tertiary colors in future paintings?
- Which tertiary mixture surprised you the most?
- Are you convinced to stop purchasing burnt sienna or sap green?

Mixing greens can be the bane of contention for many painters. You just learned how to mix bright and dull secondary colors in chapter 5. Let's go and expand upon this knowledge and mix a greater variety of natural-looking greens in the next chapter.

CHAPTER 7

How to Mix Bright and Dull, Natural-Looking Greens

It's not easy being green...
Kermit the Frog, Joe Raposo, songwriter

Is this the first chapter you are reading? Maybe you flipped through this book specifically looking for an approach to mixing greens?

If this was the case, I wouldn't fault you because natural-looking greens are a challenge to mix.

That is why I put a lot of time and thought into developing an effective way to mix natural-looking greens using the Balanced Palette System. In addition, this approach takes advantage of your knowledge of complementary colors and color bias.

But, I have a warning: mixing greens is more complex than what you have been doing up to now.

And if you haven't completed the exercises in my previous chapters, I'm afraid I can't give you a "Get Out of Jail Free" green card. That's because you *really, really* need to finish the exercises in the first six chapters before diving in here!

However, *if* you have read the previous chapters and completed the exercises, then congratulations! You are ready to mix greens!

"But I can never mix greens the way I want!" is a lament I often hear from painters. You don't like the greens that come out of tubes, and you don't like the mixtures that result from sincere attempts to mix blue and yellow.

I don't make promises lightly, but this I promise: Complete all the exercises in the first six chapters, and by the end of this chapter, you will *love* to mix green no matter your medium.

First, let's look at why greens are difficult to mix:

- Because green appears nearly everywhere in our environments, we expect it to be easy to mix.
- Like candy, tubes of paint are irresistible; the many tubes of green are no exception. After buying several greens, I remember being frustrated because none of these looked natural.
- Matching hues to the subtle differences in a landscape of multiple greens is not easy,
- There is almost no mixing-green instruction that can be applied immediately.

In the ongoing debate—*using tube greens versus mixing with yellows and blues*—I hail from the latter school of thought.

Because green is a secondary color, this mixing-greens chapter is an extension of chapter 5.

So, let's review:

- To mix bright and dull secondary colors requires knowing the *color bias* of the primary colors being used. (See pages 31–33.)
- When mixing secondaries, different color biases directly impact your results. (See page 71.)
- If the two primaries used to mix a secondary color include a pair of complementary colors, the mixture will be dull. (See pages 64–70.)

When I discovered these three core, color mixing concepts, I felt a sense of relief, release, and elation. And I never dreaded mixing greens again.

Fully understanding these principles and the information that follows will make the difference between mixing the natural-looking greens you want and mixing the greens you don't want.

Once you experience mixing greens with this Balanced Palette System I developed, I'm confident that your green-mixing frustration will decrease as your delight increases.

Our review continues:

In chapter 4, you saw how the parent colors of red and green, which are opposite each other on the color wheel, decrease in intensity as soon as a bit of one is mixed with the other, as you see below in this chromatic scale.

The parent color of red quickly becomes desaturated as some green is added. The same happens in reverse when different ratios of red are mixed with green.

Note: In this image, I've added a little white to the bottom half of each swatch.

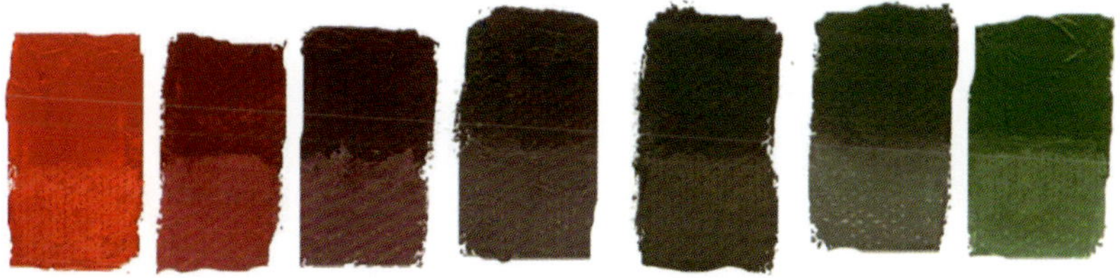

Next, let's revisit the adjectives we used to describe the color bias of yellows and blues.

They are *orange*-yellow/*green*-yellow and *green*-blue/*violet*-blue—as you see in this modified balanced palette color wheel.

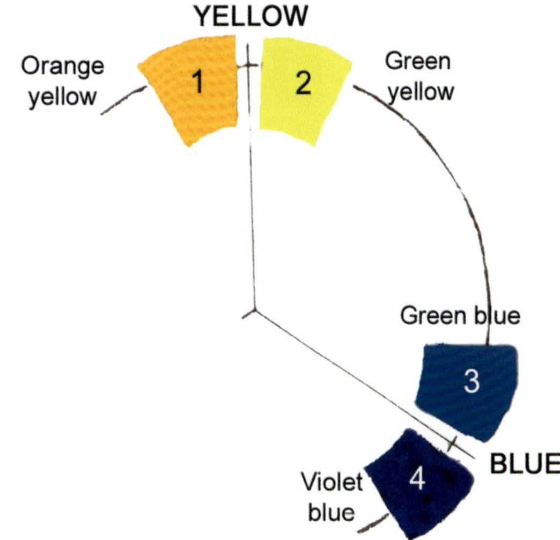

This is a good time to revisit the blues and yellows you painted when creating your Color Bias Chart in chapter 3. In this chart, you identified their color biases.

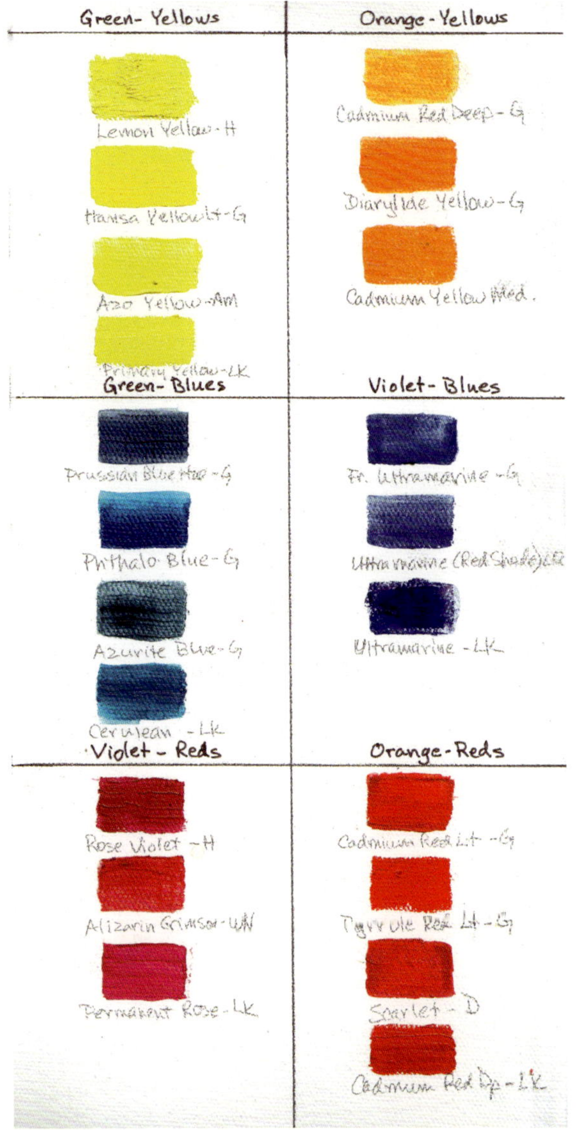

As previously stated, the best way to evaluate the color bias of your tubes of paint is by comparing color swatches side by side on a white surface. Here is my demo Color Bias Chart for your review.

When you look at it again, is it getting easier to see their differences and similarities? Do you *see* the yellows with a color bias that leans toward either green or orange? And do you *see* the blues that lean toward either green or violet, and the reds that lean toward orange or violet?

I know these questions may feel redundant, but identifying the color bias of your yellows and blues is so crucial to this unique approach to mixing natural-looking greens that I intentionally hammer it in. You will soon see why.

When you look at your Color Bias Chart, be sure your yellows and blues have been correctly identified. If you have purchased new tubes of yellows and blues since you started reading this book, I strongly urge you to add them to this chart before continuing.

When mixing greens that reflect our natural world, we need a wide variety of hues, including bright, clean greens and dull, dark greens. And now that you have identified the color bias of your yellows and blues, you will be able to mix bright and dull, natural-looking greens more easily.

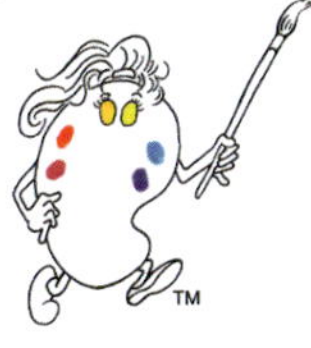

TWO COLOR TIPS:

1) Most blues on the market carry a green bias. Very few carry a violet bias.

2) For the next exercise, cobalt blue is not a good choice because it does not carry a strong, or obvious, color bias.

More About Mixing Bright and Dull, Natural-Looking Greens

In chapter 5, you discovered how a *green*-yellow mixed with a *green*-blue produces the brightest, spring like green. Using a variation of the chromatic scale, I mixed three bright greens in the sample below.

This is a dual-color mixture that creates a variety of hues with different ratios of *green*-yellow and *green*-blue.

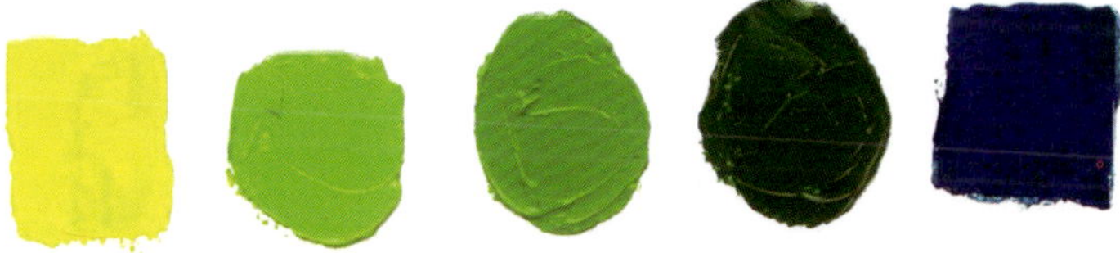

I mixed each swatch with a parent *green*-yellow and a parent *green*-blue. The swatch in the middle is an equal mixture of these two, whereas the second green from the left has a larger quantity of yellow in it, and the second green from the right has a larger quantity of blue.

These specific bright greens were created by mixing *green*-yellow-#2 with *green*-blue-#3, as displayed in this modified color wheel.

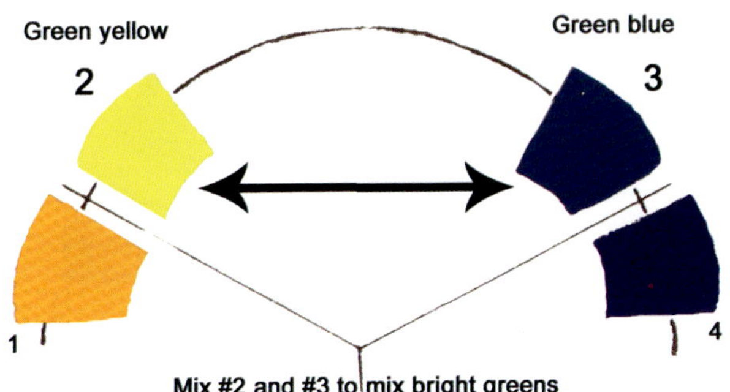

In the painting below, I mixed a variety of bright greens to convey a specific time of year. Aspen trees in the spring carry a full range of bright, clean greens. For the background trees, I needed dark, dull greens.

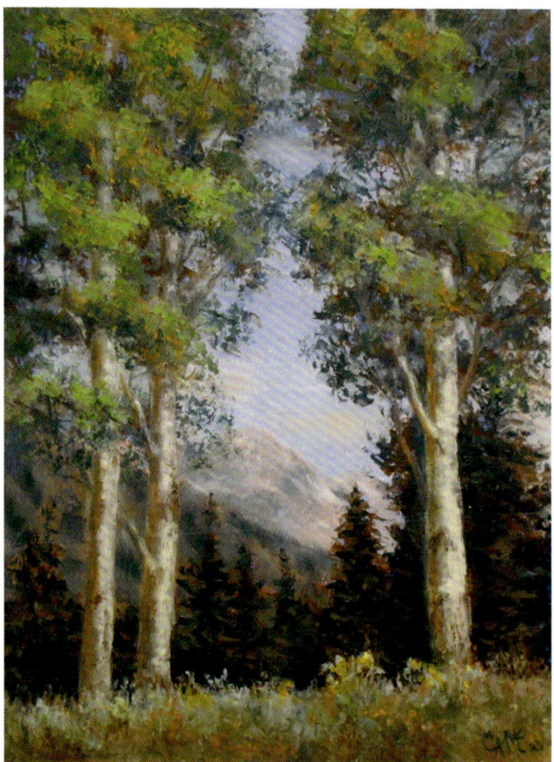

Oh Be Joyful Campground, 14″ x 11″ oil

I created these desaturated or dull greens by mixing *orange*-yellow-#1 and *violet*-blue #4.

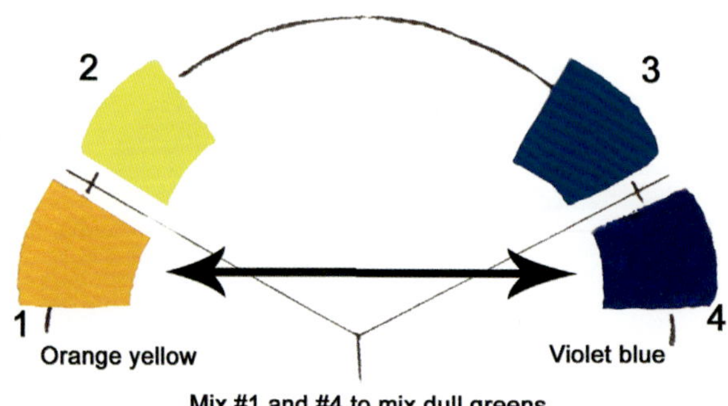

Here is a chromatic scale of dull greens created from mixing these two. Compare this scale to the one on the previous page, where neither the parent yellow nor the blue carries any red in it. Do you see how these dull greens can be used in a forested landscape?

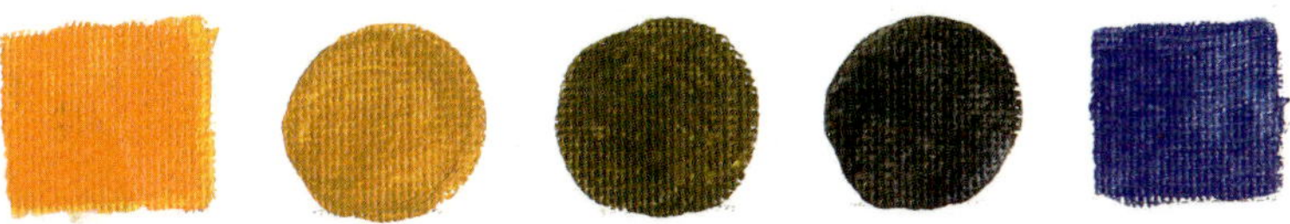

In this example, both the yellow and blue carry some red, which means that their color opposites are hard at work dulling each other when they are mixed.

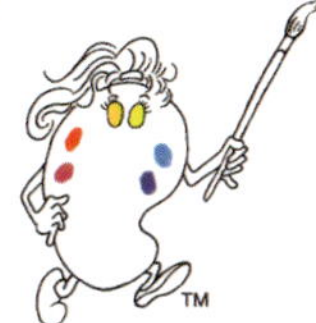

COLOR TIP: When both the yellow and blue used to mix green carry some red in them, the resulting green will not be bright and clean because you are mixing complementary colors.

Two More Natural-Looking Greens

The two previous examples demonstrated mixtures of #2 with #3 and #1 with #4, which gave us bright and dull greens respectively.

Let's expand upon this with two more yellow-and-blue combinations.

Take a guess here. What *hue* of green is going to result when you **mix #2 with #4**—a *green*-yellow with a *violet*-blue? Will it be bright or dull …or somewhere in between?

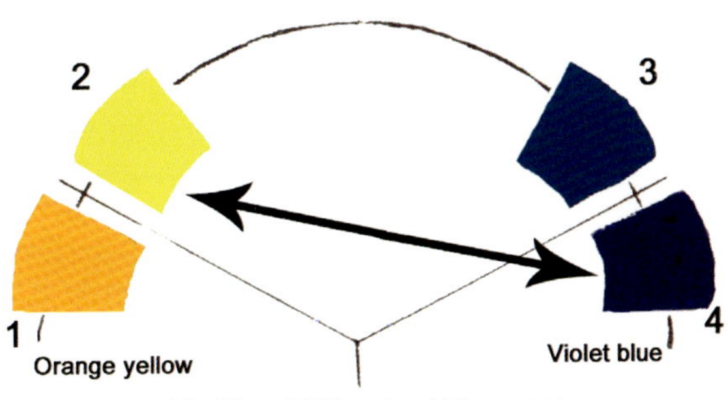

And what will your greens look like when you **mix #1 with #3**—an *orange*-yellow with a *green*-blue?

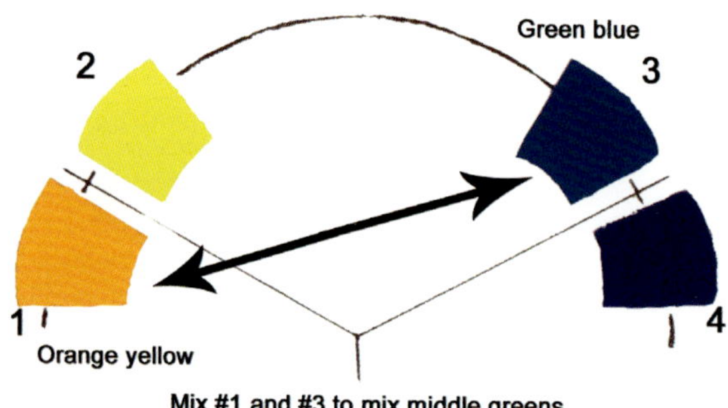

From what you know about color bias and complementary colors, you can surmise that these two additional combinations will be duller than the bright greens resulting from mixing #2 with #3, but not as dull as the #1 with #4 combination.

Let's explore all these possibilities in your own Four-Quadrant Greens Color Chart.

Exercise #8: The Four-Quadrant Greens Chart

An efficient way to maximize your ability to mix natural-looking greens is to create a color chart of bright and dull, natural-looking greens. This chart is a fun eye-opener that has been a favorite of mine and my students.

Step 1: Setting up your four-quadrant grid

Section a piece of 16″ x 12″canvas or watercolor paper into four equal sections using a ruler and pencil. The four sections will correspond to the four yellow-and-blue combinations already discussed.

Step 2: Labeling the quadrants

Label your four sections as follows:

- Quadrant A: Green-yellow-#2/Green-blue-#3
- Quadrant B: Orange-yellow-#1/ Violet-blue-#4
- Quadrant C: Green-yellow-#2/ Violet-blue-#4
- Quadrant D: Orange-yellow-#1/ Green-blue-#3

Write out the four yellow-and-blue color mixing combinations with their corresponding numbers, that is, Green-yellow-#2, Green-blue-#3, etc. Follow the examples at right. This may seem tedious, but the rewards are worth it.

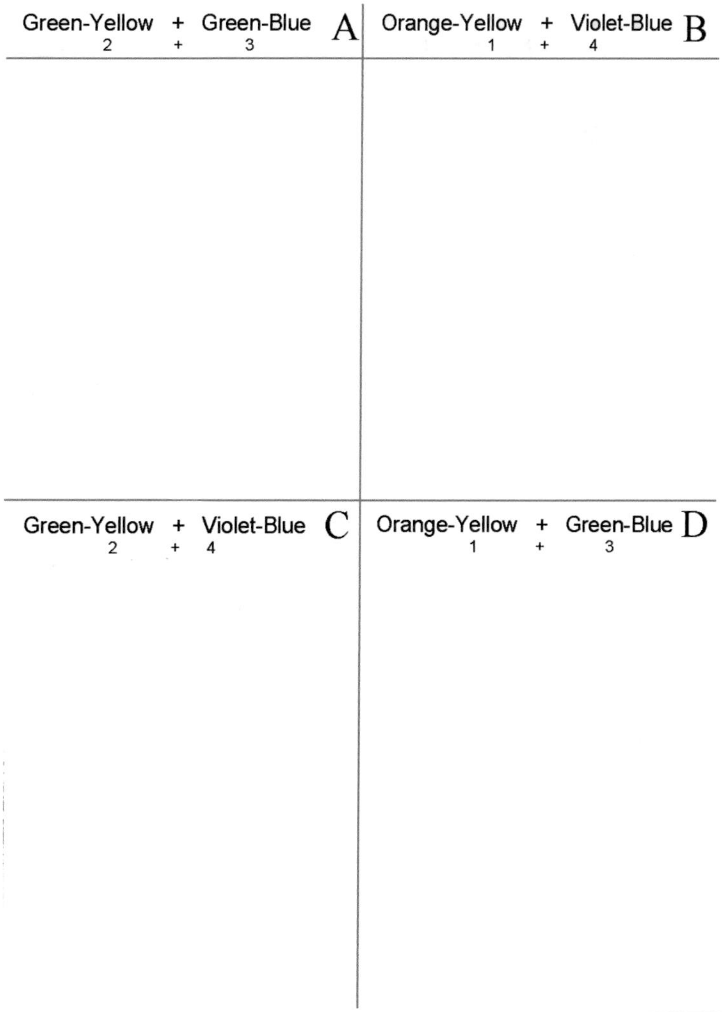

Green-Yellow + Green-Blue A 2 + 3	Orange-Yellow + Violet-Blue B 1 + 4
Green-Yellow + Violet-Blue C 2 + 4	Orange-Yellow + Green-Blue D 1 + 3

Because this chart is fairly complex, you are going to paint and mix only one quadrant at a time.

Doing this gives you a more complete reference and experience of the different greens you can mix with my strategy. Additionally, you are becoming more intimate with your tubes of paint.

Note: Remember to label each of the colors on your chart with the color's paint name and brand.

> Note: So you can see the process unfold reference the completed chart on page 100. All examples in this exercise are excerpts from my Four-Quadrant Greens Chart.

QUADRANT A

Take a look at the example below. In the first row, I painted a swatch of Hansa yellow light and Prussian blue. The second row has a swatch of cadmium yellow light and phthalo blue.

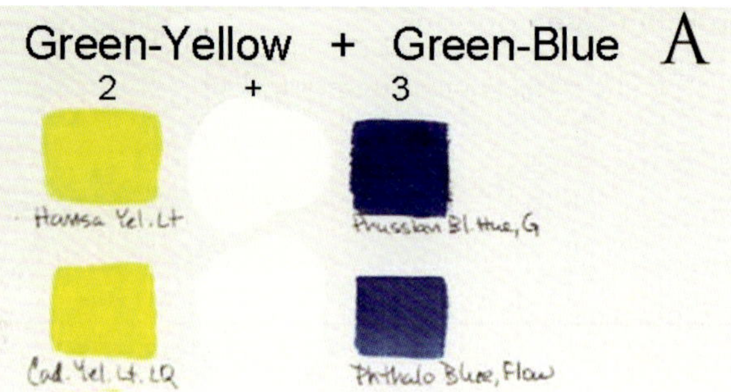

Step 3: Mixing one set of green-yellows and green-blues for Quadrant A

Line up all your tubes of *green*-yellow and *green*-blue. Select two of these as your first pair of parent colors, painting a swatch of each in the first and third columns. Then paint your second pair in the next row.

Now mix these two parent colors and paint a swatch of their mixture in the middle column.

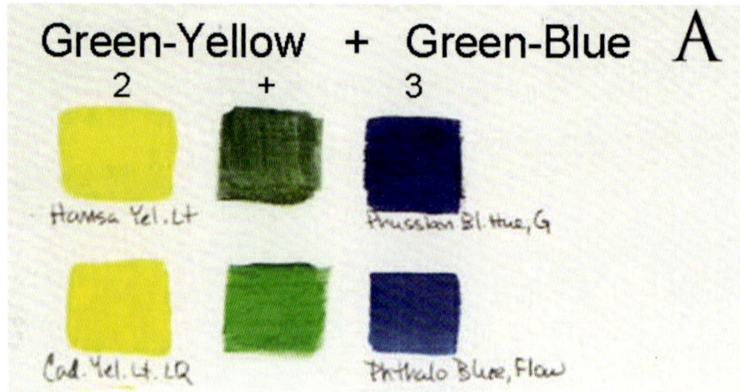

In my example, the results became two bright greens with slightly different intensities. As you proceed, pay attention to the nuance of hues your parent colors produce.

Step 4: Mixing the rest of your green-yellows and green-blues for Quadrant A

Select two more different parent colors, painting a swatch of each in the first and third columns—then mix these for your middle-column green.

Continue mixing parent colors until you have explored your entire range of *green*-yellow and *green*-blue options.

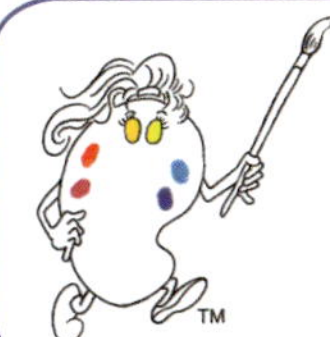

COLOR TIP: Switch your blues, as in my previous example, that is, mixing the lemon yellow with the cerulean blue. You are in store for some delightful surprises.

With this Four-Quadrant Greens Chart, you have the option to try out a variety of mixtures.

For example, below I mixed the same *green*-yellow with four different *green*-blues using watercolors. There are slight differences in hue from one mixture to the next. It's a wonderful way to experiment with your paints and discover the possibilities.

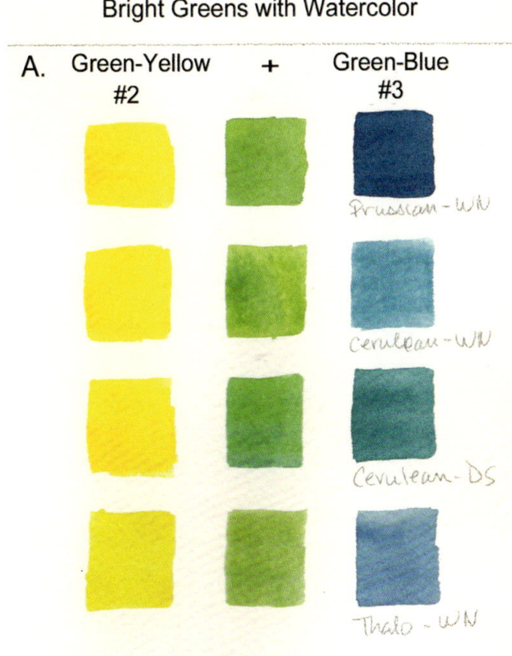

QUADRANT B

Step 5: Mixing one set of orange-yellows and violet-blues for Quadrant B

Collect all your tubes of *orange*-yellows and *violet*-blues. Select two of these as your first pair of parent colors, painting a swatch of each in the first and third columns and leaving the middle column blank.

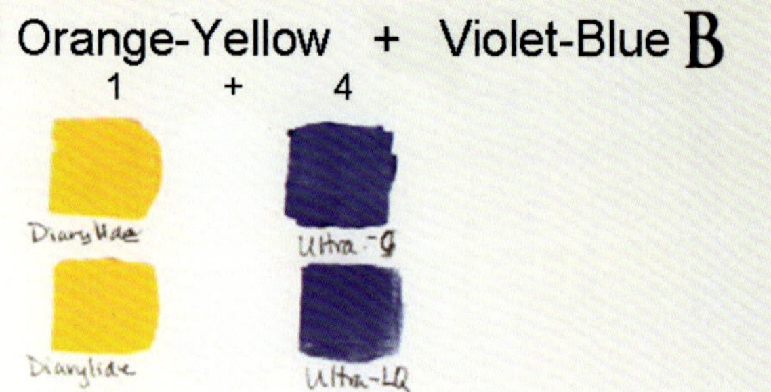

Next, mix your *orange*-yellow and *violet*-blue and apply the resulting green in between your parent colors.

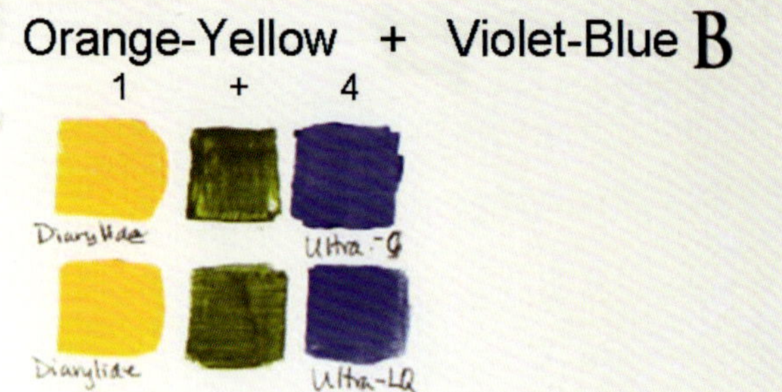

Step 6: Mixing the rest of your orange-yellows and violet-blues for Quadrant B

Select two more, different parent colors, painting a swatch of each in the first and third columns—then mix these for your middle-column green.

Continue mixing parent colors until you have explored your entire range of *orange*-yellow and *violet*-blue possibilities.

Are you addicted to mixing green yet?

QUADRANT C

Step 7: Mixing one set of green-yellows and violet-blues for Quadrant C

Gather all your tubes of *green*-yellows and *violet*-blues. Select two of these as your first pair of parent colors, painting a swatch of each in the first and third columns, leaving the middle column for a yellow-and-blue combination you have not seen before.

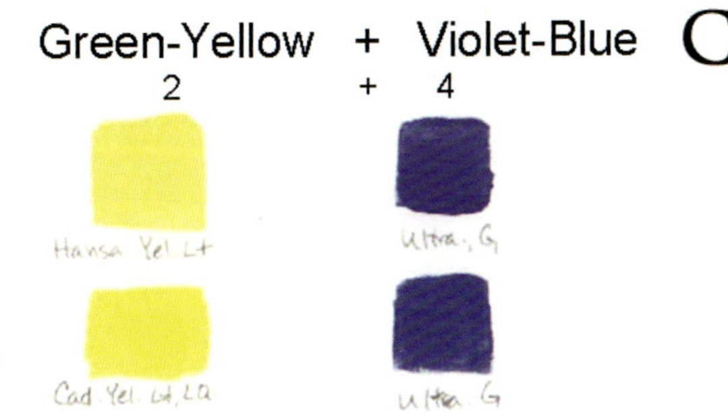

In this quadrant, only the blue carries some red in it, so your green will be duller, yet not *as* dull as in Quadrant B.

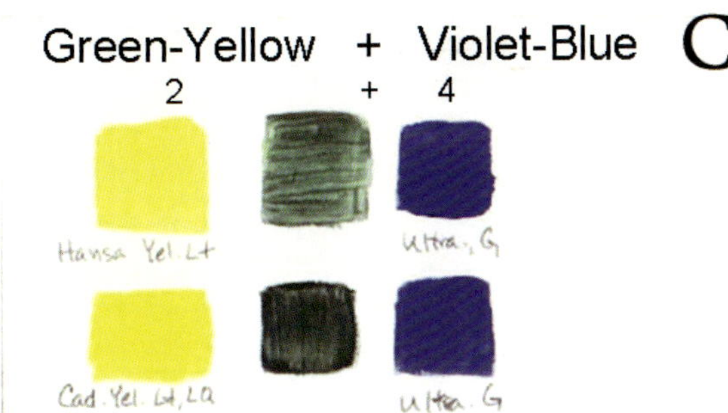

Next, mix your *green*-yellow and *violet*-blue and apply the resulting green in between your parent colors.

Are you surprised? Are you seeing the benefit of knowing the color biases of your yellows and blues?

QUADRANT D

Step 8: Mixing one set of orange-yellows and green-blues for Quadrant D

For the last quadrant, line up all your tubes of *orange*-yellows and *green*-blues. Select two of these as your first pair of parent colors, painting a swatch of each in the first and third columns, leaving the middle column for your resulting green.

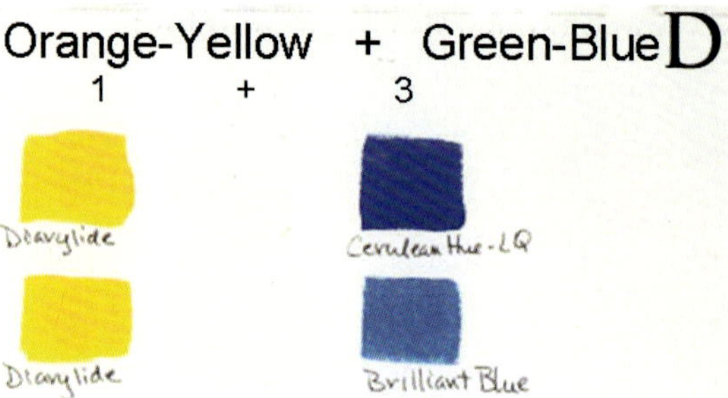

In this example, I painted swatches of diarylide yellow and cerulean blue in the first row and then diarylide yellow and brilliant blue.

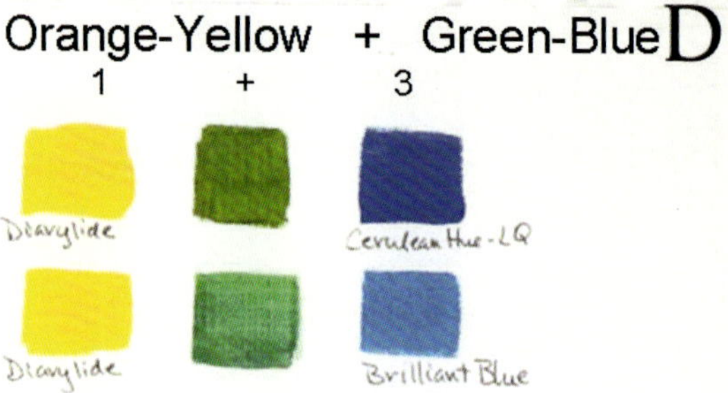

Step 9: Mixing the rest of your orange-yellows and green-blues for Quadrant D

Select two more, different parent colors, painting a swatch of each in the first and third columns—then mix these for your middle-column green.

Continue mixing parent colors until you have explored your entire range of *orange*-yellow and *green*-blue possibilities.

Nature is full of desaturated greens of various degrees, and now *you know how to mix them.* As in the greens in Quadrant C, they are slightly duller, but not as desaturated as those mixed greens in Quadrant B.

Congratulations! You have completed a challenging, yet endlessly resourceful, chart of bright and dull, natural-looking greens. You have just experienced and benefited from using the Balanced Palette System. Take a moment to study your results.

At your fingertips, you have a successful process to effectively mix natural-looking greens—without the frustration of dipping your brush into yellows and blues haphazardly and not knowing what the result will be.

When I developed this specific approach for mixing a variety of greens, I was easily able to paint the following watercolor of grapes and vines. Nature is full of an infinite variety of greens, and it's a marvelous feeling when you know how to mix them.

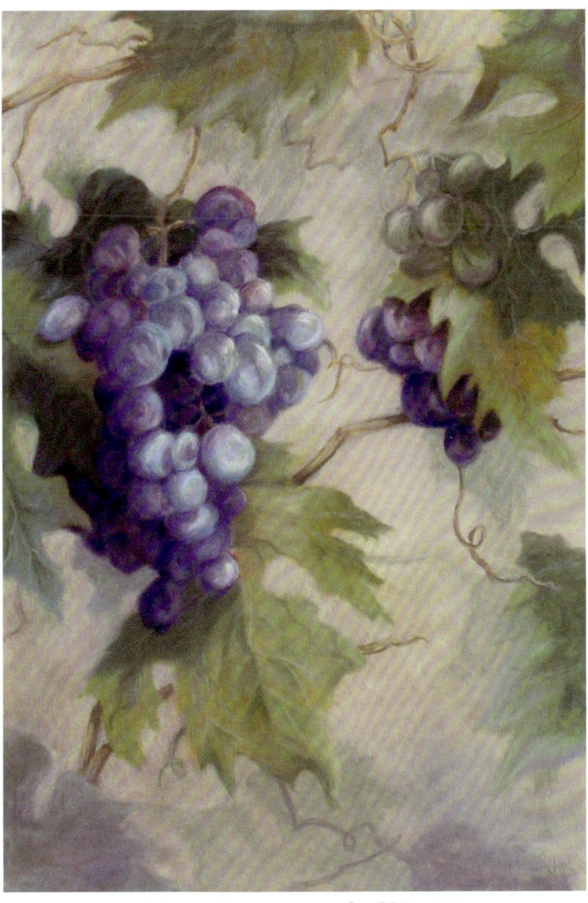

A Grape Bounty, watercolor 22″ x 14″

Below is my completed Four-Quadrant Greens Chart. Can you see how you will have as much variety as you want and need in your paintings for trees, leaves, plants, landscapes, and green abstract shapes?

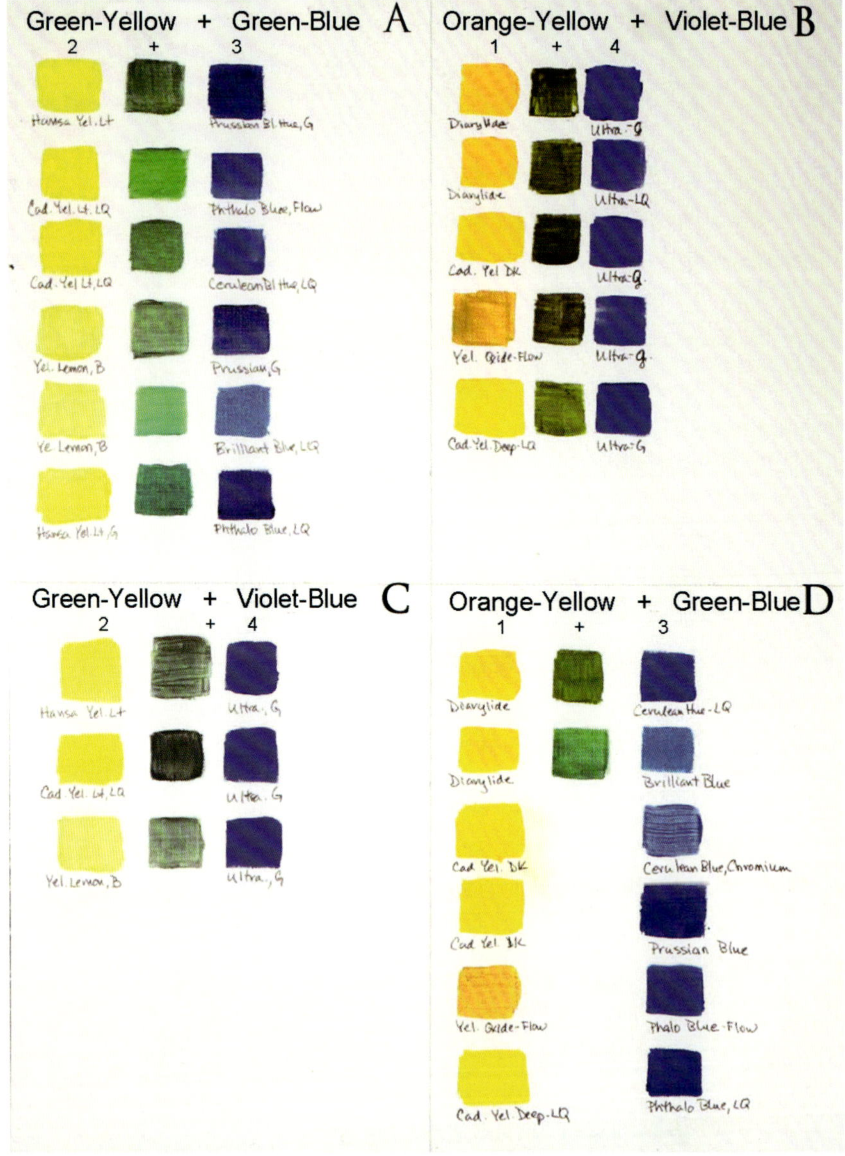

The more you experiment and try out different color mixtures in a chart like this one, the more you notice which tubes of paint and hues you prefer.

Creating this Four-Quadrant Greens Chart also helps you identify the two yellows and two blues that you will want to use for *your* balanced palette, which we discussed in chapter 3. And now that you know your yellows and blues even better than before you started, you may want to change your original choices. If you do, *make a note of any new choices* so you are ready for the next chapter, where we create your "working" balanced palette.

In my opinion, it's a lot more satisfying mixing color with the paint tubes you choose than it is following what an instructor or another artist says to do. This is why I seldom tell you the specific names of each yellow and blue; I want you to decide which ones work best for you and the artistic statement you want to make.

Greens for All Seasons

Years ago, after I created my first Four-Quadrant Greens Chart of natural-looking greens, I noticed something interesting. Each quadrant, or combination of yellows and blues, appeared to represent a different season of the year—summer, spring, fall, and winter.

Using photo software, I cropped out just the greens from my completed chart to show you what I mean. Quadrant A represents spring, Quadrant B represents fall, Quadrant C represents winter, and Quadrant D represents summer.

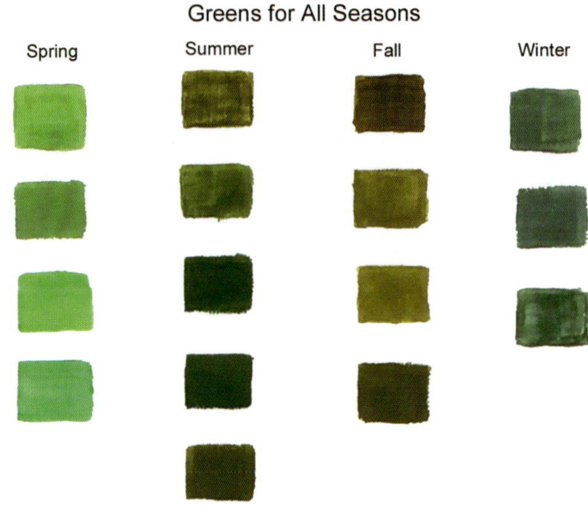

Discovering these greens for all seasons reinforced my belief in the practicality and effectiveness of the Balanced Palette System for mixing color. It eliminated a lot of color mixing confusion.

What other observations have you made as you have studied your Four-Quadrant Greens Chart?

This approach to mixing greens has opened up the flow of my painting. Now I mix a variety of natural-looking greens with confidence.

My painting *Dancing with Light* would not have been possible without developing and implementing my green-mixing strategy. Believe it or not, I didn't use a single tube of green in this painting.

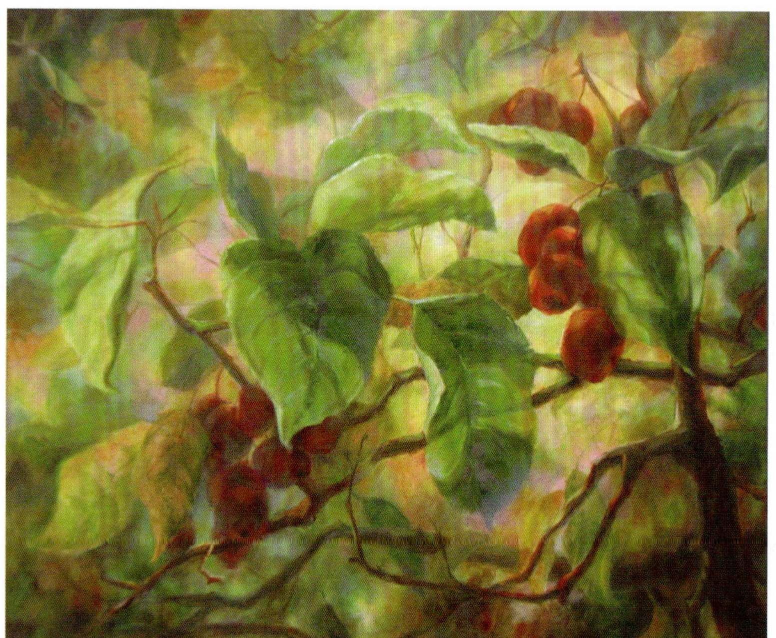

Dancing with Light, oil, 30″ x 34″

As I've mentioned, your color decisions reflect your artistic vision.

The Four-Quadrant Greens Chart you just completed is a critical foundation that gives you more confidence to mix natural-looking greens. It is also a reference tool when you need a particular green and want to remember how to mix it. So, keep it handy when you paint!

However, for this exercise, I had you mix with several tubes of yellows and blues so 1) you would start to notice which tubes of paint you prefer, and 2) you could better decide which of the two yellows and two blues you want when it's time to set up *your* unique, "working" balanced palette in the next chapter.

To decrease your number of yellows and blues and identify which ones you want for *your* balanced palette, let's create a simplified, natural-looking greens chart.

Exercise #9: The Simplified Greens Chart

Step 1: Choose one yellow-green and one green-blue that you created from your parent colors.

Pick the *yellow*-green and *green*-blue that resonates with you. There is no right or wrong decision—only what feels or looks right to you.

Step 2: Mix these into a chromatic scale

Painting chromatic scales of greens is another way to discover and explore the potential of your tubes of paint. It also increases your color mixing confidence.

Note: This is similar to what you did in chapter 4, pages 49–51.

On a small piece of canvas or watercolor paper, such as a 6″ x 8″ piece, paint a variation of the chromatic scale with the pair of yellow and blue you just selected.

Now, mix a scale of greens using different ratios of *green*-yellow and *green*-blue as shown here. Make a note of the ratio so you can repeat your results down the road.

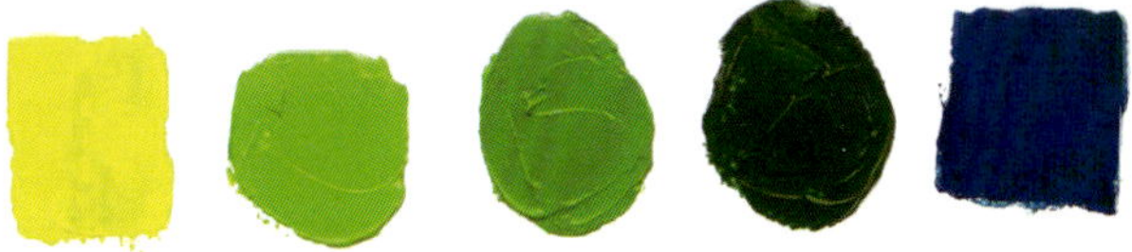

Step 3: Mix the results from Step 2 with orange

In this next step, mix an orange with each of the mixtures in the previous chromatic scale. It doesn't matter which orange you use; just try it to see the impact on your bright greens.

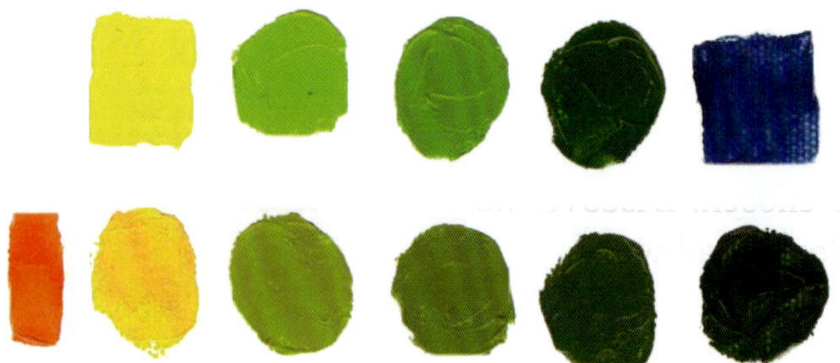

As you can see, the three green mixtures in the bottom row have become duller greens just by mixing orange. With only three colors—*green*-yellow, *green*-blue, and orange—you can mix many green variations.

Also—as you have probably surmised—when you mix green with orange, these middle three greens become a set of tertiary colors.

With just a few tubes of paint, look at the variety of greens you can get!

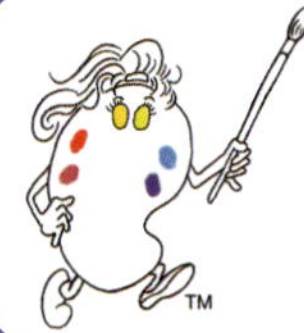

COLOR TIP: When orange is mixed with green, the green immediately becomes desaturated, or duller, as discussed in chapter 6.

Step 4: Choosing one orange-yellow and one violet-blue tube of paint

Choose your favorite pair of *orange*-yellow and *violet*-blue paint from Quadrant B.

By choosing one pair of yellow and blue that mix into bright greens, and one pair that mix into dull greens, you end up with just four tubes of paint as per the balanced palette discussed in chapter 3.

Yes, this simplifies your color decisions because you have fewer choices, yet it also gives you an abundance of mixed greens.

A possible set of paints could be Hansa yellow light (*green*-yellow) combined with cadmium yellow deep (*orange*-yellow) and Prussian blue (*green*-blue) combined with ultramarine blue (*violet*-blue).

A wonderful variety of greens can be mixed with these four tubes of paint. Then, by adding a little orange, your green possibilities expand significantly.

Experiment mixing greens with the yellows and blues you have chosen. Discover how it opens up new, colorful pathways.

By simplifying the number of paints you start with and using the above green-mixing approach, you can mix the greens you want or need with ease. Think of it as losing your driver's permit and advancing to driving on autopilot.

In this painting created with a palette knife, again I mixed a variety of greens. Within the greens, I let some of the orange show through to create a greater assortment of color. It is one way to entertain the viewer with color and texture.

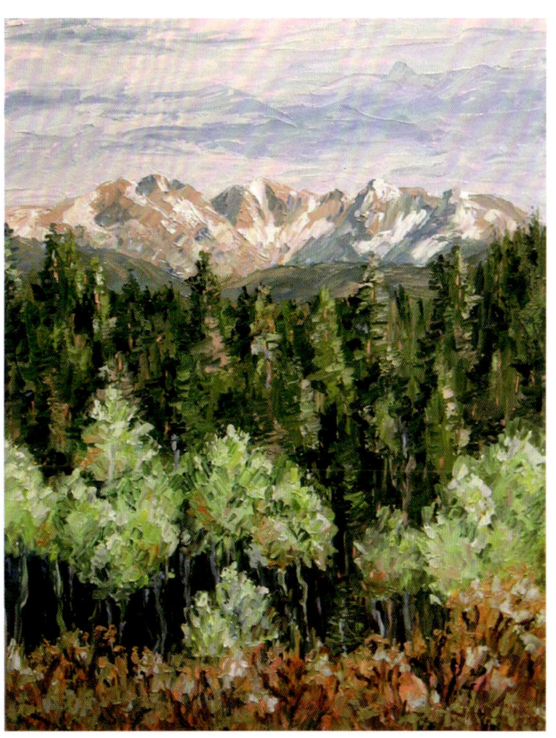

Above Vail Valley, acrylic, 14" x 11"

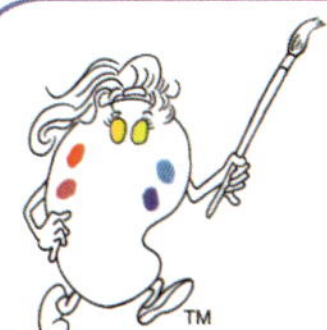

COLOR TIP: Another benefit of implementing my Balanced Palette System is that when you are painting on location, you need fewer tubes of paint to mix all the greens you want.

Are you excited about being in control of your green-mixing process and of implementing your knowledge of the Balanced Palette System?

In summary, you have reached a certain level of understanding with the following:

- How color bias impacts the results of your color mixing
- How complementary colors play a role in mixing color
- How to choose tubes of yellows and blues, and one orange, to simplify mixing your greens
- How to mix a variety of natural-looking, bright greens with a few tubes of paint
- How to mix a variety of natural-looking, dull greens with a few tubes of paint

Now that you know how to select a specific yellow and blue for the specific green you want, maybe this will encourage you to skip owning tubes of green or only having one or two in your paint box. And when you are ready to buy your next tube of yellow or blue, you'll go in knowing the color bias you need.

By being strategic in choosing tubes of paint, you will experience more color mixing success. Also, you will be less tempted to buy a seductive tube of color that you don't really need since you'll be able to create as many dazzling greens as you want.

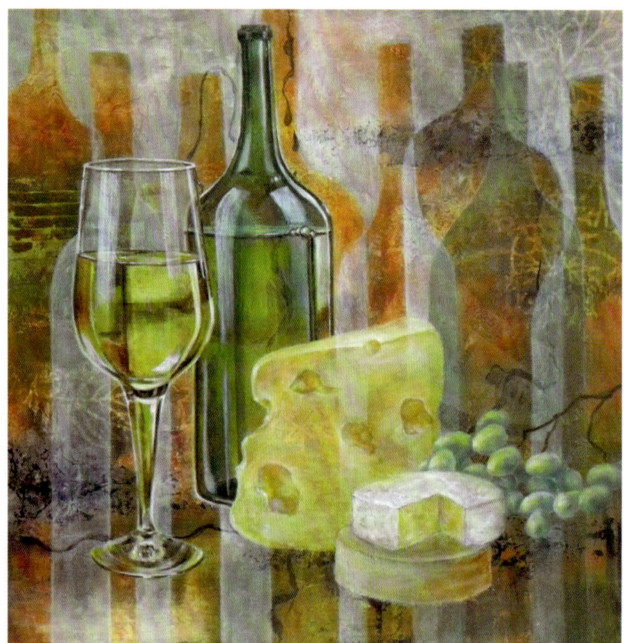

Visions of Paris, acrylic/mixed media, 20″ x 20″

Here's another example from my portfolio demonstrating how greens can be mixed easily and confidently when using a balanced palette of strategically chosen yellows and blues.

Speaking the Language of Color Mixing!

The more you paint and mix colors, the more you develop the skill of seeing the color bias of any color, which is critical to mixing the colors you want. When mixing, pay more attention to the bias of each primary tube of paint and less to its name.

For example, say to yourself, "I need a *green*-yellow for this mixture." Don't say, "I need my cadmium yellow light." When you start consciously stating the color bias of the primary you need, your color mixing will become more proficient, and you will be speaking the language of mixing color!

Questions to Ponder

- Which quadrant, or two, of greens do you prefer? Or do you like all of them for different reasons?
- Do you see how you can use these different greens in different situations?
- What was the most surprising combination of yellow and blue for you?
- Are you convinced now that you do not need to own tubes of green?

You have come a long way in color mixing confidence. Are you ready to put your color mixing into action? Have you thought about how you would place your colors onto a working palette? In the next chapter, I will give you an example of how I lay out my balanced palette.

Ideas for Future Color Charts

CHAPTER 8

Putting the Balanced Palette System™ into Action

Are you ready to start painting?

I know you just want to paint! However, before I describe how you can put your balanced palette into action, I want to review the three ways paint can be mixed:

1. Mixing on the painting palette
2. Mixing on the painting surface
3. Layering or glazing one color on top of a dried layer of color

The first color mixing approach—mixing on the painting palette—is the most common and the one you have been doing as you have mixed multiple colors for the chart exercises in this book. Hence it does not need to be reviewed.

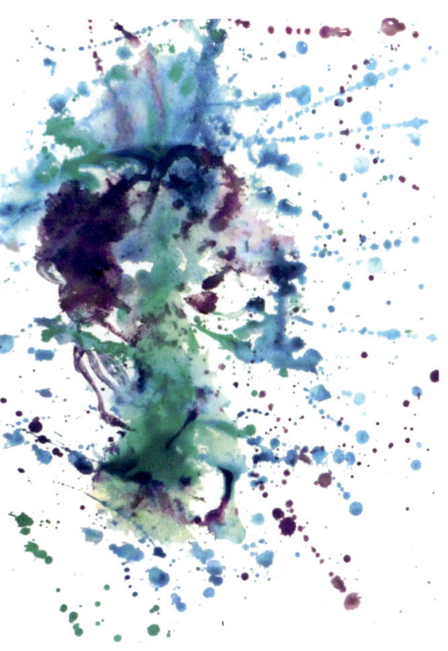

So, let's review the other two methods of mixing color.

Mixing directly on the surface of a painting is a lesser used but important approach. Earlier in my painting career, I made the mistake of not learning and not using this method. As a result, I missed out on discovering how to create interesting textures and experiencing visually exciting results.

Mixing on the surface is usually done in wet-into-wet situations as seen in the watercolor illustration on the previous page. I both splattered paint and charged a wet puddle of paint with a brush loaded with paint. The enchanting merging of these colors could not have been achieved any other way.

In this next example, I blended colors by overlapping them slightly on a dry canvas. First, I brushed on a color swatch of permanent rose, cleaned the brush, overlapped it with ultramarine blue, cleaned the brush again, and painted a swath of lemon yellow, followed by cadmium yellow medium. You can see how the colors of purple and green mix on the canvas while the paints were still wet.

Another way to mix color on your canvas or paper is by pouring different colors into or next to one another. Here is an example of one of my experiments. I poured paint from small 3″-high cups and then tilted the canvas to help move the paint around. Then I ran a comb through a couple of areas to create some interesting shapes and texture.

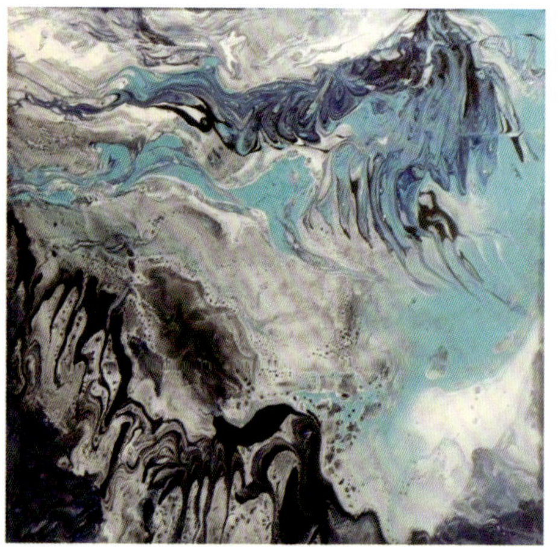

There are additional ways to exploit this way of mixing on your substrate, and I encourage you to seek out resources to learn about these techniques.

Because you've learned about **color bias** and **complementary colors**, you will experience more success getting the colors you want as you mix on a surface. Mixing colors directly on your canvas and paper also gives you an unpredictable element to the creative process.

Experiment and be curious with your medium to discover your options. It's delightful to see what happens.

A third method of mixing is layering. Glazing or layering one color over another alters a hue and is frequently used by painters as a color mixing strategy. It is an excellent way to change the saturation or value of a color.

For Step 1 of the next demonstration, I painted a bright pink flower shape surrounded by desaturated *blue*-greens. In Step 2 I showed a color change through layering by applying a layer of *green*-yellow diagonally across the lower left. In Step 3, after this first layer had dried, I applied another thin layer of *green*-yellow over the entire piece.

Do you see the subtle hue differences? Compare the left and right painted samples and decide which you prefer. Then ask yourself *why?* Or perhaps you can imagine different applications for both in future paintings.

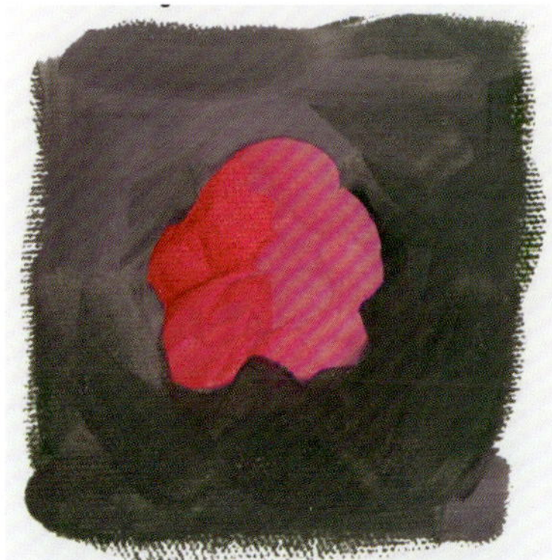

Step 1. Pink flower shape surrounded by gray blue-greens

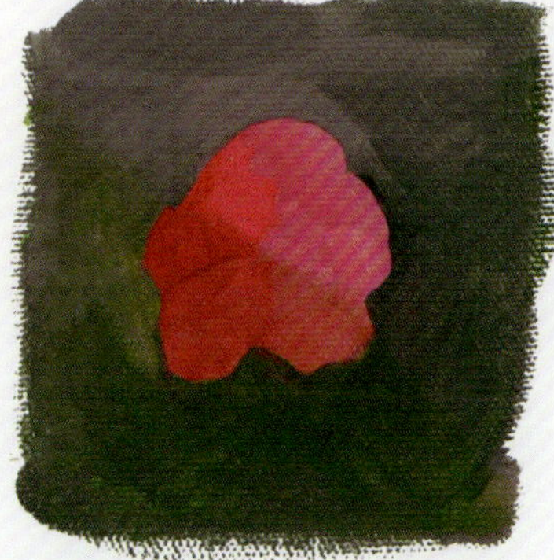

Step 2. Green-yellow layer

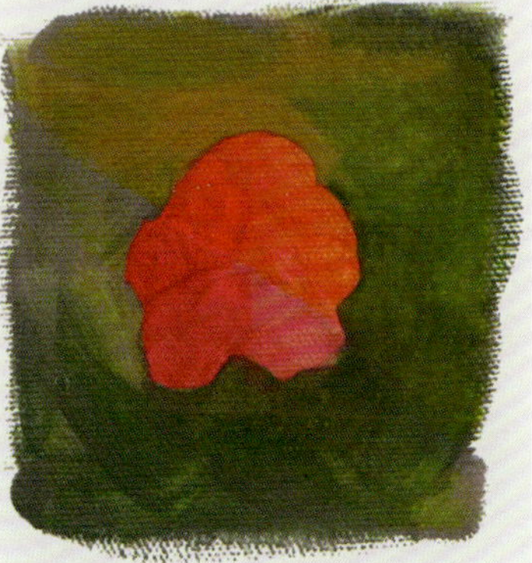

Step 3. Another green-yellow layer over the entire piece

When layering paint, I recommend using your more transparent paints, as we discussed in chapter 2. It's fascinating to see how one or two thin layers of paint can alter the original colors. Layering can be implemented in all media, but it may take practice before you feel confident doing it.

Some painters strategically use this layering technique at the beginning of their painting. In the next example, of a hat painted with watercolor, I'll show you what I mean.

Because I know how complementary colors impact each other—in this case, blue and orange—I wanted my first layer of paint to be a blue. I let that dry before painting a layer of burnt sienna—my orange—over it. I chose these two colors in this sequence because I knew they would convey a worn, leathered look. Notice the interesting interplay between these complementary colors as some of the blue remains visible through the second layer of burnt sienna.

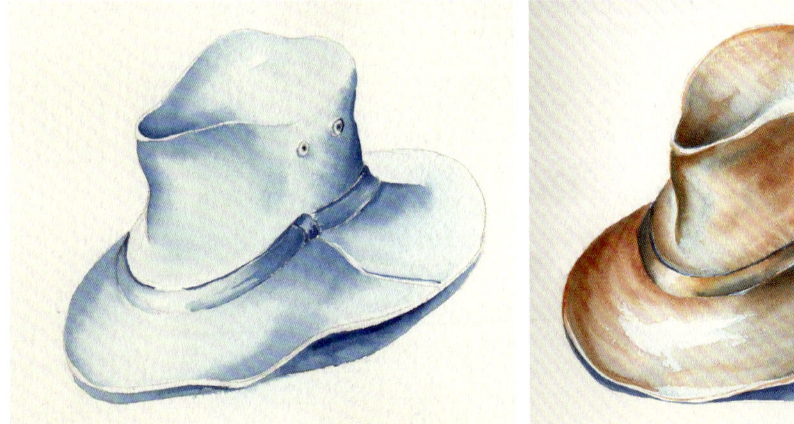

Years ago, I was so fascinated by the impact of layering colors that I created a chart I refer to, with affection, as my Plaid Shirt Chart. You can see that I listed my paints down the left and across the top. I then used a 1" brush to paint the horizontal stripes. After they dried, I then painted the vertical stripes.

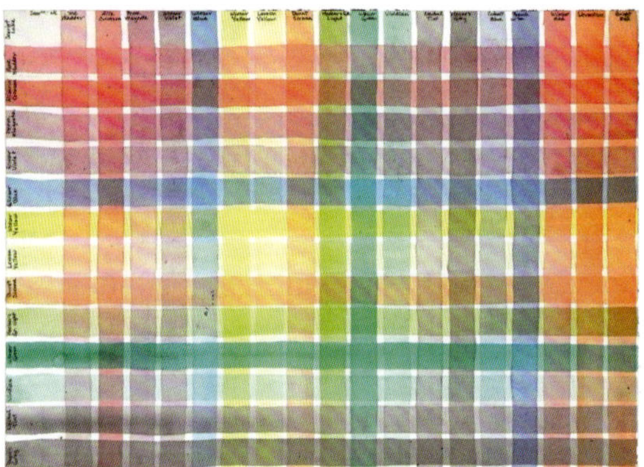

Are you seeing and experiencing the value of creating color charts?

As you continue to paint, start thinking of a chart that may be helpful to you and your artistic development. Then you can join me as a member of the "Color Chart Junky Club!"

OK, I have held you off long enough. It's time to put your balanced palette into action. What does a working balanced palette look like? How might you lay out your paints?

Process Exercise: How to Lay Out a Balanced Palette

Step 1: Translating your balanced palette onto a working palette

Deciding how to set up your working palette for painting is personal. Just like we all uniquely organize our clothes, we each have our own way of arranging our paints. However, because the Balanced Palette System has been our focus in this book, I wanted to show you how I translate my balanced palette onto my working palette.

In the left side of the image below, I have the numbered balanced palette color wheel you have been seeing throughout this book. On the right, you can see where these primaries are squirted out onto my palette. They are numbered to correspond to this graphic. **There is no *correct* way to do this.** It just happens to be how I like to lay out my paints.

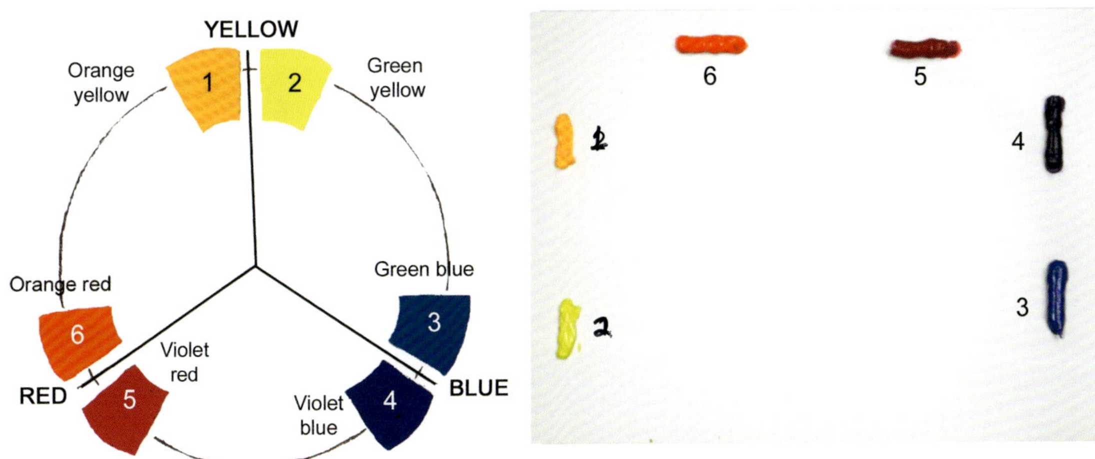

You may want to try different arrangements until you find the one that suits you because it harmonizes with your creative flow. Being left- or right-handed may also have an impact.

Watercolorists can arrange their set of primaries on their palette using the wells in their palette, making sure to leave empty wells in between for the mixed primaries, secondaries, and tertiaries. Refer to page 17 of chapter 2 for an example.

Step 2: Squirting out your colors

Grab a clean palette and the six primaries that make up your balanced palette, plus white if you work in an opaque medium, and start considering how you would like to lay out your paints or follow my layout. Squirt out about a 1″ length of each color, leaving enough space in between to add another pile of paint.

Step 3: Mixing your primaries

Wait. Don't start painting quite yet! The old adage that patience is a virtue applies here. In the previous step, I directed you to leave your six primary paints spaced fairly far apart on the palette for a reason. In the next image you'll see that I have mixed my primary pairs.

In other words, I mixed the two yellows, then the two reds, and then the two blues. I placed the pile of mixed yellows between the *green*-yellow and *orange*-yellow, the mixed reds between the *orange*-red and *violet*-red, and the mixed blues between the *green*-blue and *violet*-blue.

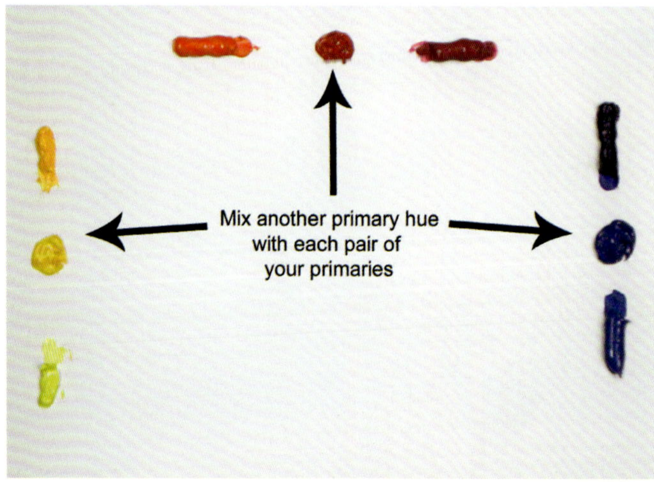

You may be asking, "Do you really do this?" Yes, I do. The mixing of primaries of the same hue family is not something commonly done, and I am not sure why.

Step 4: Continue mixing piles of paint

Next, I mix my bright secondary colors as discussed in chapter 5. I only mix the bright versions of my secondaries. You can see here where I have placed them.

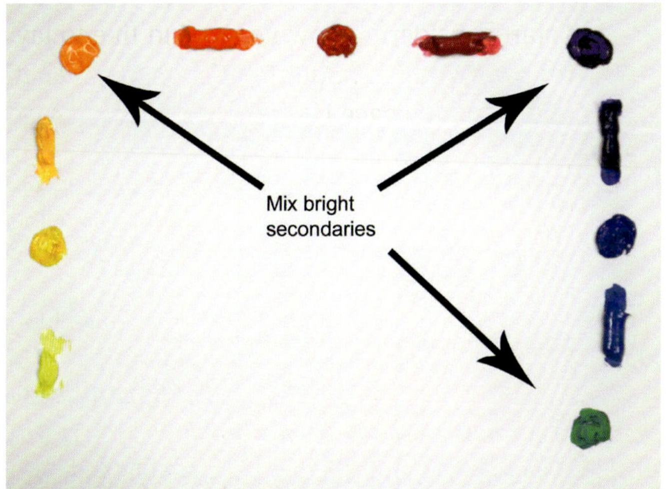

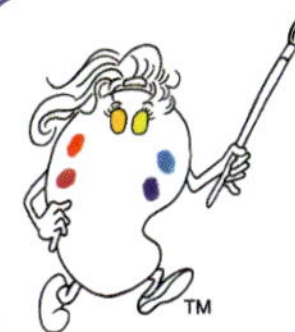

COLOR TIP: A hue can easily be desaturated, but you cannot do the reverse. In other words, you cannot change or mix a dull color into a saturated color.

Step 5: More mixing of paint to add to your palette

Next, if you want to continue setting up your palette of colors, which I recommend, you can mix your tertiary colors of burnt sienna, olive green, and purple-black, as outlined in chapter 6. I place them in the lower left of my palette.

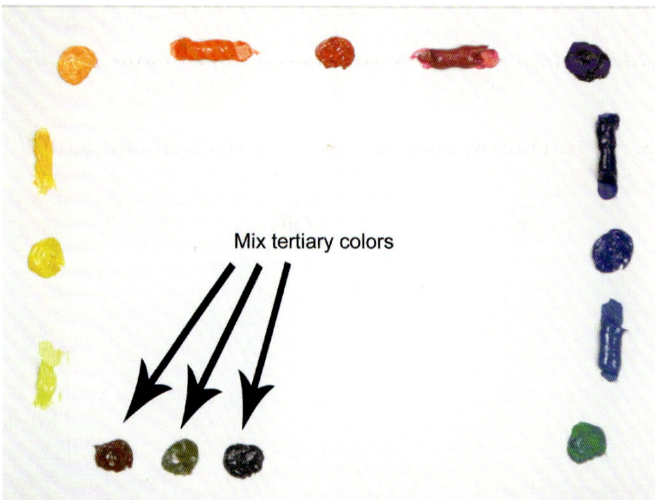

Adding these mixtures to your working palette is optional. However, I do like to premix these additional secondary and tertiary colors because my painting process becomes more efficient. Premixing does take time and can test my patience when I am starting a new painting because I just want to paint, but it really saves time down the road. Also, the rhythm of my painting is not interrupted because I don't have to stop to mix a color. I have never regretted taking the time to premix.

Variations on Your Balanced Palette

This is an appropriate time to mention what some painters call "convenient colors." These are tubes of paint we purchase even though we know how to mix them. Burnt sienna is a good example because it is a color that many of us use, and we get lazy and just want to squirt out the color from a tube. I do caution that, at this juncture, it is best to learn to mix with your balanced palette using just six colors before adding any convenient tubes of color.

Spend time mixing and painting with your set of six primaries to master their nuances and capabilities. The more you know how to mix with them, the easier it is to push their limits. Maximizing the minimum—in other words, only working with six primaries—is freeing and facilitates your confidence as a painter. At the same time, you learn more and more about your color preferences and tendencies, which leads to creating the colors that truly reflect your artistic vision.

Earlier in the book, I mentioned that you may ultimately have more than one balanced palette to experiment with or for a particular subject matter. In this table, I share the primaries I use in my balanced palettes for the three different media: watercolors, oils and acrylics. As you know, paint names vary from manufacturer to manufacturer.

Primary Colors	**Watercolors**	**Oils**	**Acrylics**
Orange-yellow	New Gamboge	Cadmium yellow medium	Diarylide
Green-yellow	Aureolin	Hansa yellow light	Lemon yellow
Green-blue	Antwerp blue	Prussian blue	Prussian blue
Violet-blue	Permanent blue	Ultramarine blue	Ultramarine blue
Violet-red	Permanent rose	Magenta rose	Quinacridone magenta
Orange-red	Cadmium red light	Cadmium red light	Cadmium red light

I do not have another set of primaries for a second balanced palette per se; instead, I tend to exchange only one or two of my primary colors. For example, I often switch my *green*-blue to a cerulean blue or my *orange*-red to a scarlet or vermilion. By the way, it is tempting to add a seventh tube of paint to your palette—that second *green*-blue or *orange*-red—but I would like to discourage you from doing so. Stick to the six primaries!

Another reason to have a second set of six primaries or a second default balanced palette may have to do with the effect you want to convey in a painting. Some painters have *all* transparent or *all* opaque balanced palettes. No matter your reason, I suggest developing your palettes consciously and with purpose.

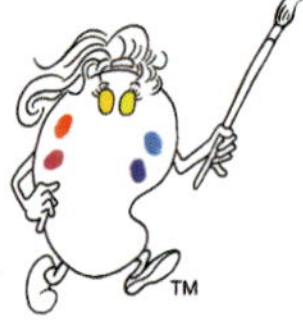

COLOR TIP: When mixing with white, notice that it will somewhat desaturate the parent color and the hue will shift slightly toward a blue hue. Painters erroneously think white will brighten a color, but it actually dulls it.

The Benefits of the Balanced Palette System

By laying out your balanced palette on a working palette, you have increased your chances of success and decreased color mixing frustration. Along the way, you have discovered some of the many benefits of this system:

- Making easier color decisions
- Understanding how to intentionally mix mud
- Increasing your overall confidence in mixing color
- Deleting the hit, miss, and wish approach to mixing color
- Understanding how to efficiently mix bright and dull colors
- Creating color unity throughout a painting with fewer tubes of paint
- Mixing the right color, which is in your mind's eye or which is the subject before you, with grace and ease
- Knowing how to analyze a color mixture that is unsatisfactory
- Bringing your artistic vision more fully into the world
- Confidently deciding which new tube of paint to buy
- Saving money by using fewer tubes of paint

Now, just go and paint! Enjoy the ride.

CHAPTER 9

The Boundless Journey of Color

Where the end of the road turns into the beginning of another

Congratulations. You are now in the driver's seat, ready to take the wheel and drive down a colorful brick road. Mixing the colors you want, with confidence and newly won knowledge and skills, leads you to the next phase of your painting journey.

Though sometimes daunting, color is also seductive. It makes us drool with anticipation to paint. It is a significant channel of expression. There is no feeling like beginning a new painting, or color chart, when you are ripe with curiosity. It's that time when anything is possible, and there is no limit to what you can discover.

I have been studying color for decades, and it still fascinates me. Color is magical and alluring. Learning more and more about its nuances and emotional impact is never tiring, which is what keeps me painting and experimenting. I love the challenges of color. I love solving them and tasting the pleasures of success *and* failure.

Color is one of the first elements in a painting that a viewer responds to. When we choose a subject to paint, it is often the colors and the light that engages us with that subject. Thus, it's imperative for painters to acquire an ongoing, working knowledge of color.

Color expertise redirects your painting process toward a state of flow and satisfaction. As in any skill development—such as mastering how to drive a car—the more we do it, the greater the sense of freedom and increased confidence.

The next turn on your path of color knowledge and confidence is learning how to *apply* the colors that will convey your visual message. Now you know how to mix the colors you need for a particular color scheme to create the mood you desire. Because of this solid foundation in mixing colors, learning how to *apply* color so it intentionally translates what is in your mind's eye will come more easily.

The Balanced Palette System has given you the three keys to mixing the colors you want:

- Seeing and identifying the color bias of your primary colors
- Understanding the impact complementary colors have on mixing color
- Mixing colors from your own balanced palette of six strategically chosen primaries

Painting—lots of painting—is the most constructive learning activity you can do to embrace and incorporate these three keys for mixing color.

Instead of worrying about the outcome of any one painting, spend your time deepening your process with painting exercises.

Experiment, push your comfort zone, and make mistakes! It is invaluable and worth the investment. Taking chances on mixing color and applying paint will teach you more than hours of cautious thought.

Design and create your own color charts and become the color chart queen or king of your area while exchanging information with fellow painters.

Most of us snatch up an instruction book or attend a workshop to find answers. We seek a magic wand or recipe to make painting easier. Even though you have been given sound strategies for mixing color in the preceding chapters, the truth is that no recipes exist—only practice and experimentation.

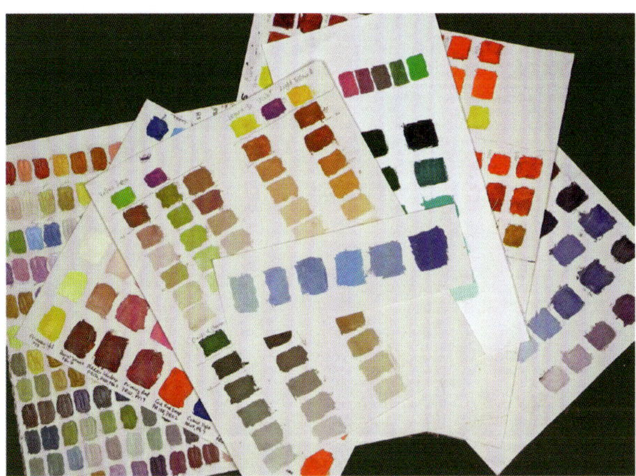

To this day, I continue making color charts. Here are a few examples:
A confident and successful professional racecar driver does not race every day but practices on the track incessantly.

While practicing, give yourself permission to make a mess! With childlike abandon, be messy as you play around with possibilities; give your inclinations a free ride. Like that racecar driver who is addicted to the smell of burned rubber and the thrill of the chase, believe in the power of your creative spirit.

Meanwhile, study the available color instruction books, online video training courses, and DVDs to learn how to make that sunset sing or that abstract painting bring a sparkle to your eye.

Being creative is a gift and a joy. Self-expression is vital for our sanity. Grab hold of it. Let color sing your soul into visions you create for yourself and the rest of us. And undoubtedly, such full measures of aliveness will take you on unexpected adventures and down roads less traveled.

Creativity is the gift to the creator, not just a gift to the audience.
—Elizabeth Gilbert, *Big Magic: Creative Living Beyond Fear*

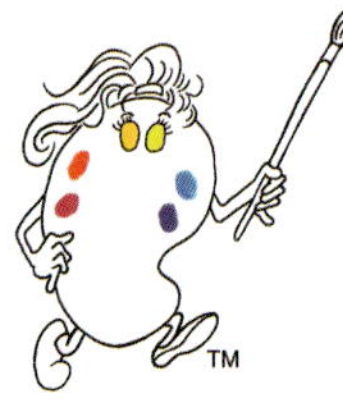

Paulette and I want to thank you for joining us as you traversed this color mixing journey. Our intent has been to increase your ability to bring more beauty into the world while jump-starting your creative expression and revealing your hidden treasures.

Together, let's bring more art to life!

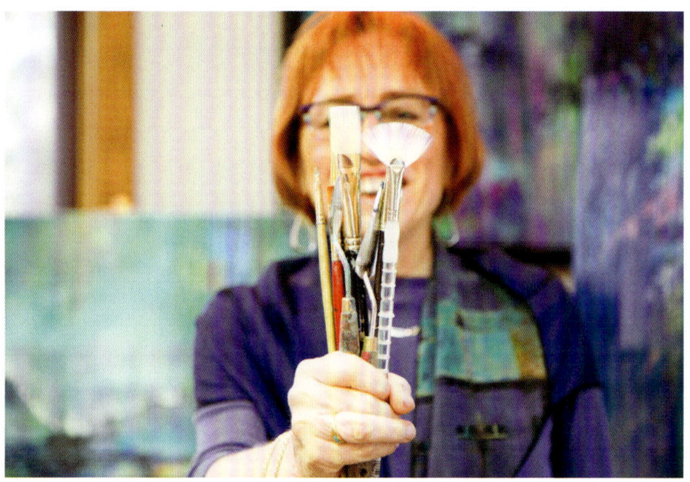

Glossary

Balanced palette. Six strategically chosen primary colors that include two yellows, two blues, and two reds.

Chroma. The degree of vividness or brightness of a hue; used synonymously with intensity and saturation.

Color bias. The hue that influences or encroaches upon a primary color, such as *green*-blue, *orange*-red, and *green*-yellow.

Color wheel. A two-dimensional circular diagram that is divided or sectioned with colors in a spectrum.

Color opposites. Colors directly opposite of one another on the color wheel. When they are mixed, the saturation of each is canceled; used synonymously with complementary colors.

Complementary colors. Colors directly opposite of one another on the color wheel. When they are mixed, the saturation of each is canceled; used synonymously with color opposites.

Complimentary. Expressing praise or giving something away at no cost. (Complimentary is included in this glossary to remind you that complementary, with an "e," describes colors.)

Desaturated. The degree of dullness of a color.

Hue. The name of a color or a family of colors, such as green, blue, or red.

Intensity. The degree of vividness or brightness of a hue; used synonymously with chroma and saturation.

Pigment: A colorant, either organic and inorganic, ground to a fine powder and mixed with a binder or vehicle that suspends the colorant and gives the paint its adhesion.

Primary colors. Colors that cannot be mixed from any other colors. They are yellow, blue, and red.

Saturated. The degree of vividness or brightness of a hue; used synonymously with intensity and chroma.

Secondary colors. The mixture of two primary colors, known as green, purple, and orange.

Tertiary colors. The resulting mixture of two secondary colors.

Value. Describes the lightness and darkness of a color. A value scale refers to the range from light to dark for every color, including white, grays, and black. Values are often numbered in scales of 0 to 10, 0–5, or 0–9.

Resources

This list of books and internet resources are ones I reference regularly or did so in the past. Most items focus on color while a few pertain to painting techniques, living the life as a creative, as well as the business of art. These represent only a small percentage of the myriad books available to artists. I encourage you to start, if you have not already, collecting for your personal library. At one time in my career, I was involved in an art book study group, which I found beneficial. Public libraries and used bookstores are good places to find more art instruction books and CDs, particularly ones that may be out of print.

Books

Albers, Josef. *Interaction of Color.* rev. ed. New Haven, Connecticut: Yale University Press, 1975.

Blaszczyk, Regina Lee. *The Color Revolution.* Cambridge, Massachusetts: MIT Press, 2012. [This is a well written history about color.]

Carlson, John F. *Carlson's Guide to Landscape Painting.* New York: Dover Publications Inc., 1973. [This is considered a classic landscape painting instruction book with many valuable tips and insights. It is so old that all the images are in black and white.]

Clinch, Moira. *The Watercolor Painter's Pocket Palette.* Cincinnati, Ohio: North Light Books, 1991.

Dobie, Jeanne. *Making Color Sing.* New York: Watson-Guptill, 1986.

Gilbert, Elizabeth. *Big Magic.* New York: Riverhead Books, 2015. [Uplifting and thought provoking, Gilbert eloquently describes living the life as a creative person and it takes to do so.]

Itten, Johannes. *The Elements of Color*, ed. Faber Birren. New York: Van Nostrand Reinhold, 1970.

Kessler, Margaret. *Painting Better Landscapes*. New York: Watson-Guptill, 1987. [This is a good how-to landscape painting book. I particularly like the section on how to paint colorful clouds.]

Leland, Nita. *Exploring Color*, rev. ed. Cincinnati, Ohio: North Light Books, 1998. [For watercolorists and one of the first books on color I owned and referenced often.]

Leland, Nita. *Confident Color*, first ed. Cincinnati, Ohio: North Light Books, 2008. [This book covers different ways to *apply* color and demonstrates several color schemes to consider for your paintings using any media.]

McMurry, Vicki. *Mastering Color*, first ed. Cincinnati, Ohio: North Light Books, 2006.

O'Brien Gonzales, Annie. *Bold Expressive Painting: Painting Techniques for Still Lifes, Florals and Landscapes in Mixed Media*, Cincinnati, Ohio: North Light Books, 2015. [Gonzales is a delightful and inspirational teacher, as is her book, which is filled with ideas and exercises designed to help you express yourself more freely.]

Payne, Edgar. *Composition of Outdoor Painting*, seventh ed. Bellflower, California: DeRu's Fine Arts, 2005. [Originally published in 1941, this is another classic on the essentials of outdoor oil painting. It is a 9″ x 6″ handbook, which makes it small enough to take on location.]

Pressfield, Steven. *The War of Art*, first ed. New York: Grand Central Publications, 2002. [If internal obstacles to success ever cross your path, you may find this little gem helpful.]

Quiller, Stephen. *Color Choices*. New York: Watson-Guptill, 1989. [Though Quiller's color wheel is complex, this book contains several good exercises to assist in understanding and applying color schemes.]

Sarback, Susan, and Paula Jones. *Capturing Radiant Color in Oils*, first ed. Cincinnati, Ohio: North Light Books, 1985. [Sarback studied with Herman Hensche, who studied with Claude Monet. She teaches how to see and use color from these two famous colorists' perspectives. I consider Ms. Sarback to be an excellent instructor.]

Stanfield, Alyson B. *I'd Rather Be in the Studio: The Artist's No-Excuse Guide to Self-Promotion*, fourth ed. Golden, Colorado: Pentas Press, 2019. [A step-by-step guidance for ambitious artists who relish time in the studio but are ready to share their art with a bigger audience.]

Internet Resources

There are many art related resources available to us at our finger tips. Here are a few that I recommend you investigate as per your needs and desires.

Alyson Stanfield's blog at ArtBizSuccess.com: Offers hundreds of free articles on her blog to help artists with their marketing and business. Check out her podcasts while you're there.

Artists Helping Artist at www.Blogtalkradio.com/artistshelpingartists: Is a weekly blog radio show hosted by artist Leslie Saeta. The show covers a wide range of topics related to the business of being an artist. She often interviews artists to learn about their artistic journey and process.

Carolyn Edlund's blog at www.ArtsyShark.com: Publishes artist portfolios and features articles on the business of art. Topics are art marketing, sales strategies, selling art online, and other essentials for artists who want to launch or grow a successful small business.

Golden Paints Newsletter at www.JustPaint.org: Features a variety of articles about the use of art materials, acrylic painting techniques, color and how best to use their products.

Munsell color blog at www.Munsell.com/color-blog/: The Munsell Color Company continues the legacy of Albert H. Munsell (American, 1858-1918), who gave us the color system most artists use today.

Renée Phillips' blog at www.Renee-Phillips.com: Known as "The Artrepreneur Coach," is a mentor and career advisor for artists helping them achieve their fullest potential. Her blog contains hundreds of articles and several e-books on the business of being an artist.

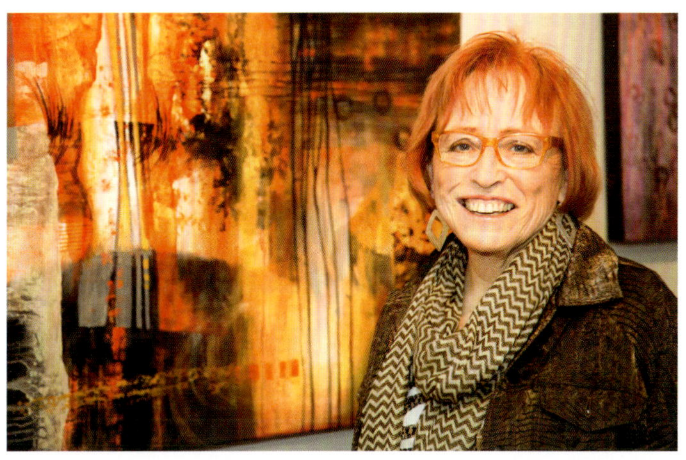

About the Author

Carol McIntyre's first run-in with the "color police" happened when she was in kindergarten. Her teacher asked the class to choose two favorite colors that went well together. Carol spoke up. "Red and orange," she said, whereupon the teacher declared, "No, these two colors *don't* go together!"

According to Carol's mother, Carol arrived home quite distraught. Years later, Carol felt exonerated when her color expertise proved this uneducated teacher incorrect. Although Carol made art during her adolescent years, at twenty-one she shut the door. After majoring in art her first year in college, she switched majors when she came to believe that she could not make a living as an artist.

With a master's degree in educational psychology from Indiana University, she pursued careers as a school psychologist, a corporate trainer, and an independent training consultant. At age thirty-six, she traded in her corporate business suit for an artist smock. For fifteen years she had kept the creative vault shut until her beloved late mother-in-law, also an artist, introduced her to watercolor. Carol was a duck swimming in water—literally and figuratively.

Her second run-in with the "color police" came two years into her self-directed painting education. Carol asked a well-respected art instructor for feedback on how she mixed and applied color. He said, "*You* understand color." Dumbfounded to speechlessness, Carol was perplexed because she knew this wasn't true. Her hours of frustration around learning color mixing and application proved that his statement could not be true. Like every beginning painter, mixing colors to produce a color she wanted often resulted in mud.

Undaunted, she went on a hunt for color theory art classes. Living in a large US metropolitan area with many local art centers, she was shocked to learn that these classes didn't exist. Finally, she found one class in the graphics department at the University of Minnesota. She convinced the professor to let her attend as an unregistered older student. This sixteen-week course opened up the doors to information Carol had been seeking. To further her studies, she began acquiring color books and CDs whenever one crossed her path.

Soon after, she observed her fellow artists struggling with color, even as they bought into the myth that applying color is more intuitive than learned. So, once Carol saw the benefits of her color mixing using the Balanced Palette System™, she started offering workshops. She developed her signature system because no other approach existed. Painters in her classes went from skepticism to high fives as they learned to understand and apply Carol's straightforward and accessible approach to color.

Carol is a national, award-winning artist who has served as president of the Minnesota Watercolor Society. She is a signature member of the Transparent Watercolor Society of America and holds associate memberships with the Oil Painters of American and the American Women Artists. She was the cover artist of *Watercolor! Magazine* and has been a show judge and curator. Carol's online color mixing video course—*Acrylic Color Mixing Made Easy!*—was produced by Craftsy, the high-quality international online video company, and it has reached over 3,200 painters.

After her paint brushes and palette knives, her second favorite tools are carpentry and power tools. In the summer, you can often find her painting and writing at her sacred mountain cabin in Colorado.

The antithesis of a "color police officer," Carol is passionate about teaching beyond the "what" to the "why-and-how" of color. Because her concepts are easy to remember and apply, artists become empowered as they unleash the voices of their creative power.

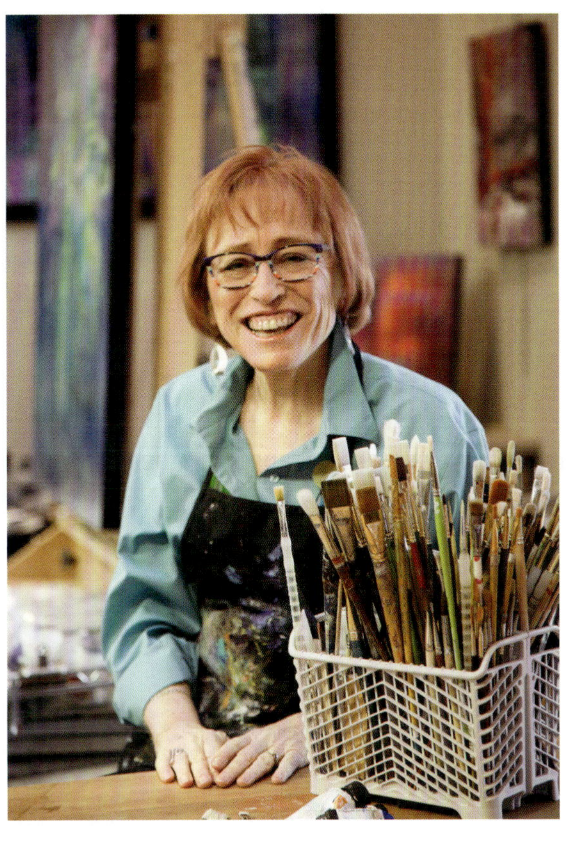

How to Work with Carol

Experience how Carol's *Balanced Palette System*—which is revolutionizing the way painters see and mix color—can inspire you to unleash your true color expertise. With her straightforward and accessible approach to color theory and color mixing, she hands you the keys to stop making mud as you successfully mix the colors you really want.

As an Instructor

After attending her classes, you will return to your studio with:

- An increased awareness of three, key concepts to mixing the color you want
- A clear understanding of how to create your working palette for mixing any color you need
- Simple strategies and solutions for mixing clean colors

Having taught in a wide range of venues—from undergraduate college art courses to art centers and senior centers—Carol knows how to reach adult students of all types and ages through her sense of humor, compassion and expertise. She teaches private lessons, workshops, and online.

As a Coach

As an artist, Carol knows how to really listen to your questions and concerns while observing your artwork to understand your developmental stage as a painter. With this information, she can help you move to the next level.

Carol's perceptive and informative coaching style gives you recommendations to meet your personal, artistic goals. Her critiques provide you with concrete feedback and guidance in a relaxed and safe setting.

One-on-one coaching sessions are conducted via an online video program or in-person.

As a Speaker

For artist groups:

Your audience will experience Carol's enthusiasm, clarity, and humor as she demonstrates a variety of painting skills related to mixing color in all media. Painters learn how to avoid mixing mud, how to mix natural-looking greens and/or how to set up a working palette for mixing the colors they want.

Through her signature approach to mixing color, known as the Balanced Palette System, Carol shows artists how to see and mix color with confidence. They are able to apply what they learn immediately. Among the art organizations she has worked with are: the Minnesota Watercolor Society, Pastel Society of Colorado, Edina Art Center and Pikes Peak Watercolor Society.

Ms. McIntyre has also served as a judge and juror, as well as leading effective group critique sessions.

For non-artist groups:

Your audience will be taken on the artist's creative journey as Carol invites everyone to take a peek into her artistic process. Experience Carol's unique perspective on what's behind the canvas, as she unfolds her journey in discovering and pursuing her passion. Carol's training in psychology, along with her experience as a fine artist, connects the bridge between the mind and the brush in an accessible, down-to-earth style. She has spoken to chambers of commerce, AAUW meetings, teacher unions, professional conferences, and conducted multiple corporate training programs.

> *Your teaching style is very effective and enjoyable. I love your answers to students, especially your sense of humor and positive reinforcing attitude! For example, "I wear paint attracting cloths in my studio" and "slobs are welcome." Thanks for sharing yourself with your knowledge and talent.*
>
> —Rhonda McNab, student

Interested in having Carol teach, coach or speak to your group?

Ask about her availability through email or visit her website.
Carol@carolamcintyre.com
CelebratingColor.com

Follow Carol:
Blog: CelebratingColor.com/blog
Facebook: Facebook.com/colormaestro
LinkedIn: LinkedIn.com/in/carolmcintyre
Instagram: Instagram.com/colormixingexpert
Pinterest: https://www.pinterest.com/celebratecolor/

Mailing Address: PO Box 88073, Colorado Springs, CO 80908

Acknowledgments

Though the act of writing is a solitary activity, the final creation and production of a book depends on a supportive and competent team. It took several years, and lots of nudging from fans and students, to provoke me into writing this book about mixing color.

Despite several false starts, it was the encouraging and unsolicited testimonials from my online color students who gave me the final push of confidence to pull this off.

We have all heard of editors, but how many of us have actually experienced their artistry? My editor, Ariane Goodwin, was a passionate and proficient conductor who was able to arrange—and rearrange—my words while interpreting my essential meanings so that they turned into an accessible book. I grinned and sometimes groaned with gratitude every time I received her edits and rewrite suggestions. Her magical love of language made this book a reality.

A core group of friends and fellow artists offered input and cheered me on from the sidelines as they provided emotional sustenance. Special thanks go to Ann Grasso, Helen Hiebert, Dona Miller, Barrett Edwards, Mary Adoretti, Terry Genesen Becker, Molly Wingate, Johanna Cellucci, Dianna Cates Dunn, Irma Jennings, Hilary Serrao, Mary Jane Pappas, and Doug Haug.

Other team members included six "beta readers," who enthusiastically and honestly gave me invaluable suggestions on my fledgling manuscript. They were Sharon Brown, Sharon Boyle, Liz Coyle, Carolyn Dennis, Barbara Haviland, and Wayne Ralston. In addition, Ana Melikian's gracious and generous private and group coaching calls helped keep me on the right business and marketing track.

An enormous *Thank You* goes to my husband, Bob, who quietly and knowingly nodded, listened, hugged, coaxed, witnessed my fears and hurdles, and then hugged me some more with a steady endurance I needed. Lest I forget, he regularly arrived in my office or studio with plates of food to assure my engine stayed fueled. He too believes in the mission and potential of this labor of love, especially after being the first editor of the earliest draft.

Given we live in an online world, I would be remiss if I did not mention the valuable information I received via webinars and online classes offered by Joan Stewart, Judith Briles, Amy Collins, John Kremer, Tom Antion, and several others. They all provided nuggets to help me learn about the book publishing industry.

In addition, these gifted people played vital roles: illustrator Shawn Rubbin, webmaster Marta Goertzan, copy editor Tom Locke, line editor Janice O'Kane, graphic designer Julia Evans, and book printing consultant Karen Stuth.

Finally, endless thanks go to all the students and painters who study color and sent me encouraging words of support, some of which I captured in this book. Their questions added richness to both the process and the end result. With deep gratitude, this book is for you!